JAN STEWER

Jan Stewer
A WEST COUNTRY BIOGRAPHY

Douglas J. Cock
WITH A PREFACE BY J. C. TREWIN

MOONRAKER PRESS

To my wife

© 1980 Douglas J. Cock
First published in 1980
by MOONRAKER PRESS
26 St Margaret's Street, Bradford-on-Avon, Wiltshire
SBN 239.00192.3
Photoset by Quadraset Limited, Radstock
Printed and bound in England at The Pitman Press

Contents

	PREFACE BY J. C. TREWIN	*page* 7
	INTRODUCTION	9
ONE:	THE BIRTH OF JAN STEWER	12
TWO:	THE GROWTH OF JAN STEWER	19
THREE:	FROM A CARRIER'S VAN	30
FOUR:	FROM PAGE TO STAGE	39
FIVE:	TEACHER	54
SIX:	PLAYWRIGHT, ACTOR, EDITOR	65
SEVEN:	THE LATER WRITINGS	78
EIGHT:	THE IMMORTAL JAN STEWER	96
	CHRONOLOGY OF WORKS	100
	INDEX	101

Acknowledgements

My first acknowledgement must be to the surviving children of A. J. Coles: Mr Harry Coles, Mrs Mary Bowey and Mrs Joan Lilley. They have told me much about their father with what I can only describe as affectionate candour, and have given me free use of some of his unpublished memoirs. Without these sources of information, this biography could not have been written. I must add, however, that the book is mine and I take full responsibility for any of its weaknesses. The judgements and assessments of the writings and performances of 'Jan Stewer' are mine especially.

I am also grateful for much useful information passed on by the late Stuart Keen (whose early death was a loss to all cinema-lovers) concerning what may be described as the non-Jan Stewer side of A. J. Coles's career.

I must in particular express the very great debt I owe to Mr J. C. Trewin for so readily contributing his kindly and discerning Preface.

Preface

This is a tale of two people who were, almost indivisibly, one: A. J. Coles, the creator, and Jan Stewer, the creation. The whole of the west country knew Jan Stewer, one of the most relishing dialect humorists the regions of Britain have ever produced. Fewer knew A. J. Coles, though no one who did would forget him; Mr Cock has now succeeded redoubtably in flashing up the man and the mind behind the legend.

I heard Jan Stewer's name often when I was a boy in the remotest peninsular village of South Cornwall. Loyalties down south were very strong, and Jan was a Devonian; even so, he had become a familiar folk-name in our village, and later, on going up-country, I found out what he meant to the most unlikely people. Those were days long before television, and radio was in its cat's whisker dream: yet everyone knew Jan.

Dialect humour can be an acquired taste; many sins have been committed in its name. Still, Jan was always above the strife, and his work remained true, wise and friendly—just to what extent we can see now from Mr Cock's incidental extracts. Unprofitable as it is to guess what may or may not endure, I hazard that Jan Stewer, of all west-country writers, will speak to the generations ahead.

During the summer of 1931, while a journalist in Plymouth and closely involved with the local repertory theatre, I called on an excited Bernard Copping (then producer of the Plymouth Rep.). 'We've got a prize coming,' he said. 'A new comedy by Jan Stewer. That will bring them in.' It did; and I remember clearly the first-night applause and Jan responding to his author's call, something rare at the Rep. Though there was always a good cast in those days—Copping was shrewd and selective—dialect comedy was never easy. Many first-class players have failed to include it in what used to be called the 'professional pack'; I recall one excellent actor at Plymouth—in the years before *Barnet's Folly*—who was so foxed by any form of dialect that it became an agony to listen to him. Cast him for any convenient peer, and all was well. What he would have done with Jan Stewer, I cannot imagine. As it happened, the *Barnet's Folly* company, though it had at least one Scots girl—who played Hettie—could put up a likeable show: Jan was fortunate enough to have a Devonian, Leslie Sanders (a young man then, with a natural eye for crusted character) as George Growsell. This was the part Jan would make his own: it was a delight one day to see his name on posters at the heart of the West End; of all theatres, the Haymarket.

This is a diversion, for playwriting was only a second string to his bow. But because my own life had been round the theatre I found, on meeting Jan at last—and by then it was late in his career—that we talked of it as a matter of course. We met annually, for a long time, at the conferences of the West Country Writers' Association. Waveney Girvan, its founder, was managing director of two publishing firms, one of which, Westaway, concentrated on books from the west of England, especially Somerset, Cornwall and Devon. Wisely, it began to specialise in Jan Stewer, for whom Girvan had a great and lasting admiration. Year by year, as we entered the conference hotel, Jan would be there, an early arrival sitting contemplatively in a corner and waiting to give Girvan his annual lesson in dialect: resolute master, devoted pupil.

It was at an early Bath conference that Jan, with a very straight face, produced the pun ('bone-ash'—Beau Nash) that, heard in its context, drew the longest laugh I remember in Association records. Invariably, when Jan was about, laughter accompanied him like an escort; but sometimes, away from the crowd, he could look oddly stern and lonely. I seem to understand him better after reading Mr Cock's affectionate, candid, and searching book.

We met last, unexpectedly, during the interval of a play at the Crescent Theatre in Birmingham, of which his daughter and son-in-law were prominent members. He was an old man, but his eyes were as bright as ever and his voice still had that unmistakeable warm glow. That night, going back to London, I kept on thinking of a writer who, more than anybody of his time, was the popular voice of a region and would be remembered, with gratitude and laughter, long after his death. Always, at the back of my mind, there beat a few lines from Kipling:

> For their work continueth,
> And their work continueth,
> Broad and deep continueth,
>   Greater than their knowing!

J. C. TREWIN
Hampstead

Introduction

An unaccompanied little boy sat entranced in the old Station Hall at Westward Ho!, the seaside near his home town of Bideford. Some kindly strangers gave him chocolate caramels from time to time but his eyes never left the stage, for on it was the most delightfully comic creation he had ever seen. Though he had for some years chuckled over the writings of Jan Stewer, he was now seeing him on stage for the first time, and years later, in full manhood, he was to speak of the occasion with the same reflected glory that one of an earlier generation might have evinced when saying 'I saw Dan Leno'. On this occasion he did not merely chuckle, he laughed loudly, helplessly and immoderately. Jan wore a top-hat, an ear-to-ear beard, a mop of unparted hair, a frock-coat, breeches, leggings and hobnail boots. He carried a stick in his right hand and held a red cotton handkerchief in his left, and walked with a bent, slightly comical gait. He told some of the tales the little boy had already read, but now they came to life as he changed his features for every character of which he spoke. He even changed his expression for each of the names in the chorus of 'Widecombe Fair', making the variations identical each time; and he sang his own uproariously comic song 'Out Come Mother and Me'. There are benighted northerners to whom the name Jan Stewer signifies merely the second name in the 'Widecombe Fair' chorus, but the little boy had heard and read about Jan Stewer long before he knew that song.

A few years later, when he was eleven the little boy went down with mumps. It was then that he sent his first fan letter: he wrote it in the Devonshire dialect, and referred to himself as 'a li'l tacker'. He was rewarded with a copy of the song, inscribed: 'Douglas Cock from Jan Stewer, A. J. Coles, 20.2.26.'; and a letter which read: 'My dear Douglas, Thank you for your letter which I read with much pleasure. I am sending you a copy of "Out Come Mother and Me" which you can have for your own. With all best wishes, Yours very truly, A. J. Coles, Jan Stewer.' The recipient has had several letters since that time—the last was in 1964—for the correspondents were later to meet and exchange jokes in Coles's

Pathfinder caravan home at Tedburn St Mary, near Exeter. The letters all carry the same two signatures—save one signed only 'Jan'—and the handwriting for the two names is entirely different: one is that of a cultured man of the world; the other that of a working farmer of the old school, whom one can almost see laboriously pressing the pen hard on the paper as he performs the unaccustomed task. All the letters have been kept but it is the first that is the most treasured. It came from a house in Torquay which was later bought by a Mr Charlie Bindon on the condition that it retain its name of St Ewer which, though converted into flats, it did. A parson once asked A. J. Coles's son Harry, a solicitor who practised and retired in Torquay, in all seriousness, who this obscure saint was.

A. J. Coles's alter ego was known far beyond the boundaries of the west country. For sixty-four years his Devonshire-dialect narratives appeared regularly in the *Devon and Exeter Gazette* and the *Western Weekly News*, and, for some twenty-four years, in the *Western Times and Gazette*.

Of course, most counties have regional funny men who tell comic stories in the vernacular, but A. J. Coles was in a class of his own, perhaps the only genius in that particular field. John Betjeman said he was to be numbered amongst the great understanding humorists, citing as parallels such writers as Barry Pain and W. W. Jacobs.

At one time, A. J. Coles rented a room over a grocery store in Sidwell Street, Exeter. It was here that he wrote his stories and books, and rehearsed new sketches or parts aloud—often until the early hours—free from interruption or the fear of being a nuisance to others. Here he kept rare old dialect writings and books long out of print, works of reference, thousands of cuttings, diaries, programmes of past events, photographs, letters from readers all over the world, manuscripts, and half-written plays, which stretched back over forty years. One May night in 1942, immediately the 'all clear' had sounded after a blitz on the city, he hurried back to this room to find nothing but a hideous, contorted heap of smoky bricks. All his irreplaceable treasures had gone, along with table, desk, chairs, typewriter, cupboards, carpets, gas stove, electric kettle, teapot, and at least three pipes. He turned round, his spirit boiling and a fund of scorching curses on the end of his tongue against such a blind and stupid fate, to come face to face with an elderly man. Being only slightly acquainted with him, Coles did know that this man had a delightful home filled with the sort of treasures most men only dream about and asked him how he had fared in the blitz. The dazed-looking old gentleman replied 'What you see me stood up in is all I have left in the world.' A. J. Coles suddenly felt ashamed for he, at least, had his home left.

As a result of this blitz, only a few newspaper cuttings and theatre programmes stored elsewhere remain, a loss which rendered the writing of his biography less easy than it would otherwise have been. I am indebted to Coles's family not only for filling in some of the blank spaces, but also for a level of co-operation without which my task would have proved impossible.

But an even greater difficulty presented itself to me. Coles became identified, to a degree otherwise unknown in my experience, with the character he created. He was proud of the fact that he was known as Jan Stewer. I once overheard a bank clerk, doubtless with great correctness, call him 'Mr Coles', but somehow it sounded all wrong. I have overcome the problem by what may seem a clumsy expedient, but which seems to me the only possible one. When I refer to him as Coles (or A. J. C.) I shall use the past tense. When I am referring to Jan Stewer—particularly as he appears in the stories—I shall use the present tense, for Jan is undoubtedly one of Devon's—nay, the country's—great immortals.

This, then, is the story of a unique and many-sided personality. To begin at the beginning, as Dylan Thomas wrote in *Under Milk Wood*.

>'Twas like this-yer.

ONE

The Birth of Jan Stewer

Albert John Coles, the creator of Jan Stewer, was born in the middle of a Woolwich drawing-room on 14 March 1876, during a meal. His mother was carving the joint when, realising what was about to happen, she went hurriedly into the next room. This took place in the married soldiers' quarters at Woolwich Arsenal where his father, a master gunner when he retired, was then an artilleryman.

The date is important for an understanding of Coles's highly complex character. Victoria had been on the throne for thirty-eight years and was to reign for a further twenty-five; Harry Lauder, an entertainer whose art Coles greatly admired and with which his own had strong affinities, was four years old. When the Queen died in 1901, the subject of this biography was a struggling young schoolmaster in a remote Devon village. Stories in the Devonshire dialect signed 'Jan Stewer' had been appearing in the local press for about a year and were already receiving favourable comment. The pseudonym was to become a household name in Devon within a few years, and later much further afield than that. Cornwall and Somerset were to claim him as their own, and books in the name of Jan Stewer were to be read all over the country. He was to see his features caricatured in popular and, as he was later to observe, in some cases expensive journals. He was to see his name in large letters on London's Underground, and receive prolonged applause in a well-known West-End theatre after the first night of a play he had written himself and in which he played the principal part.

He was, then, in part a Victorian, a fact which accounts for his strong disciplinary attitude towards his children and a firm belief in himself as the paterfamilias—had he been born some decades earlier, he might well have exercised the unbending and puritannical authority of a Mr Barrett of Wimpole Street. But he also lived through the reigns of Edward VII, George V, the uncrowned Edward VIII, and George VI, and a considerable part of the reign of our present queen. These were all distinctive eras with their own special emphases or impacts, and he was, in some measure, the child of all of them, living through three big wars, participating in the First

1. School House, Puddington, where A. J. Coles lived as a young school-master.

2. A. J. Coles, c. 1915.

World War and losing a son (though not through combat) in the Second. By nature highly impressionable, he inevitably developed a complex personality, never losing the sternness associated with the word 'Victorian' but enjoying Edwardian society and the sophistication of later years.

He became a devotee of the Victorian and Edwardian music-halls, which strongly influenced his superb one-man stage shows. (Like those earlier performers, he had no microphone and was his own script-writer.) He played in Shakespeare and Chekov. When he was thirteen, there was born in Walworth, London, the greatest clown of all time, Charles Chaplin. Coles fell in love almost instantly with the pathetic little tramp figure shuffling across the small square screen of the early silent film, and was easily reduced (such was his highly emotional nature) to helpless laughter or tears. Throughout his long life he remained, as his children have testified, essentially a Victorian and the sternest of disciplinarians—the permissive age, which he just missed, and the more bizarre offerings of the London stage, would not have met with his approval. He revelled in the Aldwych farces, and once wrote a play in the same genre in which he brilliantly played a Ralph Lynn-type part.

A. J. C. was his father's second child by a second wife, (his first wife having died while he was in service in Mauritius). The original marriage had produced two little girls, Mina (Wilhelmina) and Louie, and A. J. C.'s mother also had two other children, Harry and Bertha. The family lived for some time in Kent, where A. J. C.'s father was in charge of one of the martello towers (round towers built on the coast to watch for the approach of Napoleon, and at that time still in use), and A. J. C. and his elder brother Harry were both inveterate jokers, going down the narrow Kentish streets and playing the old boyish prank of tying cotton to door knockers, pulling it and running away. They also kept up a more or less continual cross-talk, like that of Morecambe and Wise but without the aid of a script. They always called each other 'Mocus', the origin and precise meaning of this strange name remaining a secret to this day. But when one said to the other 'No mocussing', it appears to have meant 'No messing about'. Nobody else called either 'Mocus' without the penalty of a thick ear.

Brought up in a strict Anglican tradition (they were choirboys when in Kent) the two brothers' native levity would sometimes get the better of them and border on the profane. A. J. C. would announce his intention of going to early Communion by saying to Harry 'I'm going to church for a gargle', or Harry would say 'I went into the Abbey for an hour's quiet contemplation'. (The Abbey was the name of a pub in Torquay.) But there were more sombre moments. When A. J. C.'s father was stationed in Dover Castle, coastal wrecks were a common sight. On these occasions, when ships were in terrible trouble off the coast of Hythe, the inhabitants would make a human chain in an attempt to reach the survivors as they tried to come in on the great rolling waves. A. J. C.'s father was often part of this chain, and this was the case when, on one occasion, a Swedish boat was in trouble and A. J. C., then a little boy, was watching. He saw a big fair-haired fellow swimming and waiting for a wave to throw him where he could be rescued, and as he trod water, an enormous barrel, part of the cargo, hit him on the head and he disappeared. It was a sight which A. J. C. never forgot.

Too much should not be made of the apparent paradox that Jan Stewer's creator was born in Woolwich, for his parents were dyed-in-the-wool Devonians. They were both children of Devon farmers, a fact which Coles may have had in mind when he made Jan say, 'As fur as I remember, one of the Luxmores married one of the Tappers—or whether 'twas tother way round I waun' be sure.' 'The Family Tree' is the name of a short piece in his penultimate book *On The Moor of a Night*, and in it Jan confesses that tracing the Stewer family tree is too tortuous a task for him to underake:

But my Ann have fathomed out all the whole pedigree manys a time, or her thinks her have. Her loves doin' it, and I've knawed her take bes' part of an aivmin' and half the night to prove that me and Em'ly Sparkes be vorty-second cousins. The trouble is, 'tis just as likely to turn out to be sixty-vorth; and I've knawed when it have bin as much as ninety-sixth.

Without getting into such tangles, suffice it to say that in the Cullompton area were two families, the Coles and Stephens, and A. J. C.'s wife, Florence Stephens, was his first cousin. She was the eldest child of a large family, having three brothers and three sisters; her father and A. J. C.'s mother were brother and sister. Albert John Coles married Florence Stephens in Exton parish church (her parents' farm being in the parish) on 7 January 1901, the couple having met when he was eighteen and she was twenty-three. Her mother, a widow at the time, lived at Exmoor, where A. J. C. came visiting his cousins. He had intended marrying Florence on 1 January at the turn of the century, but although he put in the banns she would not at first agree, apparently being assailed by doubts. His eagerness is understandable, for early photographs show her to have been a young woman of outstanding beauty. In retrospect, her reticence may be pardoned: theirs proved to be a happy marriage, although (as will be seen) being the wife of A. J. Coles was not always easy.

They had four children. Harry was born at Poltimore, when A. J. C. was the village schoolmaster there, on 1 February 1903. Colin was born at Poltimore on 7 September 1904. He lived only thirty-five years, dying on

10 April 1940 after being in hospital for three months following a severe attack of rheumatic fever. He had joined the Territorials at Exeter when the threat of a second world war was looming, and became a sergeant. Mobilised the day war broke out, he went under canvas between Paignton and Totnes where he contracted influenza which developed into pleurisy and double pneumonia. A. J. Coles, in spite of his Victorian strain, was no believer in deep mourning or frequent visits to family graves, and his attitude was 'Let there be no morbidity at Colin's funeral.' Colin being in the Sportsman's Platoon of the Fourth Devons, was given (shortly after the birth of his sister Mary's first child) a full military funeral at Exeter Higher Cemetery.

Mary, the third child of A. J. C.'s marriage, was born on 16 August 1907. When she grew up, she often accompanied her father's renderings of his own comic songs and appeared in dramatised forms of some of the monologues, as did her sister and two brothers. I recall seeing A. J. C.'s two daughters, who inherited their father's gift of mimicry, with him in the sketch version of the census-paper monologue, Joan giving a delightful impression of a little girl having trouble with a public recitation which ended in tears. This performance was after the Second World War, in the Glenorchy Congregational (now United Reformed) Church, Exmouth. Mary also inherited, from both her parents, an indomitable and determined spirit. She was christened Mary Adeline Jenny Coles, and her brother Harry came up with the intriguing suggestion that she might have been so called because their father was an ardent admirer of the actress Adeline Genee, the toast of Edwardian London. I prefer her own explanation, that she thus preserved her father's initials. It is in keeping with his strong streak of vanity; for his next child, a daughter born on 28 December 1910, was called Joan St Ewer Coles. Said Mary: 'He'd have called us all St Ewer if he had his way.'

It was for Colin's sake that in 1927 his father bought Poole Farm (five miles from Exeter and less than half a mile from what became the caravan village of Pathfinder, which was to be A. J. C.'s last home). They changed the name to Five Mile Farm—one is almost surprised that he didn't rename it St Ewer Farm—and here the whole family lived, save Harry who was by this time in practice in Torquay.

However, all this lay in the future when A. J. C., a young man in his early twenties, arrived in Puddington near Crediton. He had left school when he was just fourteen, and was, it is believed, a messenger boy until he had enough money to join his father's regiment. A year or two later he was invalided out due to a weak heart which lasted him for nearly ninety years.

His association with the army was of value to the young schoolmaster; he had attended an army school and taken further education. Thus with a bicycle and no money he turned up as an assistant teacher at Bristol, and it was with unmixed delight that he heard the children he was to teach speaking in the accent made known to him by his mother.

In those days, Puddington's population was about 200. It had a church, a chapel, a school and a general stores; the nearest pub was the Black Dog, two miles away in the next parish. For telegraph, doctor, weekly bank or policeman, the inhabitants were dependent on Witheridge, three miles away, They had, however, the choice of three railway stations—Tiverton, Crediton and Morchard Road—each about eight or ten miles distant. Twice a week, by walking about two miles to the turnpike, they could pick up the carrier's cart for Tiverton. It was often a tight squeeze, and often meant sitting on a sack of potatoes while nursing someone's basket of eggs in one's lap; but mild scandal and native wit made the journey seem short.

A. J. C.'s new position brought him a small schoolhouse and £75 a year so that, still a bachelor, he was better off financially than most of the farm workers whose children he taught. Two years later his salary was increased by about £2 a week, which meant he was now in a position to marry. But for the first two years he lived alone in the small stone house in Puddington. It was not unattractive in appearance; lighting was by oil or candles, water came from the village pump, the bathroom was a movable galvanised tub on the cobbled floor of the scullery, and sanitation was provided across the road in the school buildings.

Even in those early days, he organised amateur entertainments. He produced a monthly magazine recording events of school and village life, which was cyclostyled on sixteen quarto pages stitched into a brown-paper cover, the writing being first done on wax sheets by the top boys and girls in the school. The circulation of the *The School Bell* just reached three figures. His daughter Mary retained four copies, although two of them are the same. The following is an example of one of the covers:

School Bell
October 1900 No. 9
Price One Penny
By taking a quantity:—
Half-a-dozen for 6d.
12 for 1/-
Special terms for quantities
of 100 and upwards
Printed on an
Ellams Duplicator

>at the "Bell" Printing and
>Publishing Offices,
>Fore Street, Puddyngton
>(opposite the Town Hall)
>and Cathedral

The articles gave a good insight into the way the school was run. An inspector's report says: 'This is an excellent specimen of a country school. The children are very regular in attendance, keenly interested in their work and making very good progress in all subjects. The teaching is energetic and intelligent. Premises and apparatus have been much improved.'

The last page, headed 'The Philosophy of Uncle Ned', was devoted to a few notes in the Devon dialect, and when a copy of the magazine found its way to the then well-known editor of the *Devon and Exeter Gazette*, Mr G. F. Gratwicke, he wrote to the young schoolmaster asking if he would write a full-length dialect story on the same lines for the *Gazette*. The request both scared and attracted A. J. C., but that week, over several bleak February nights when most of the villagers were going to bed (at about nine o'clock), he hammered out a story. He was free from interruption and the temptation of radio or television; these were days when magic lanterns were considered worth as much as threepence to see. A. J. C. decided to keep the authorship of this first effort a secret lest people said rude things about it: the pseudonym 'Jan Stewer' was chosen from the famous 'Widecombe Fair' chorus because 'Jan' for John was typically Devon. When the story was finished he carried it into Tiverton to post it to avoid curiosity at the village post office, and as he dropped it into the letterbox he told himself he would hear no more about it. He was wrong. There was no rejection slip (he was paid 7s. 6d. for it) and the very first of the Jan Stewer stories appeared in the *Devon and Exeter Gazette* on Friday 9 March 1900.

The Boer War was in progress at this time and that issue, like those immediately before and after it, were full of the relief of Ladysmith. The front page, despite the raging of a major war, consisted wholly of advertisements. The main headlines were: 'Lord Dundonald's Entry into the Town.' 'Scenes Never to be Forgotten.' 'Speech by Sir George White.' It was reported that in the House of Lords the Lunacy Bill had been read a third time and passed. It was stated that half-hour services of intercession for those engaged in the war were being held every Friday at St Stephen's Church, Exeter. Shaped boots were advertised at 10s. 9d. a pair. Somewhere inside the paper appeared a contribution headed 'The Talk at Uncle Tom Cobley's Club. Wrote by Jan Stewer.' It began:

I'll tell 'ee thease time all as I kin min' a' t' vurst meetin' as us iver 'ad, though 'tis so long agone now, I mos' vorgets 'cep what I 'as wrote down in t' gurt buke what us kips t' records o' t' club. Uncle Tom ca's 'un t' blue buke 'cause 'tis parlymentary like, though why ur should ca' 'un th' blue buke when we've a'got a 'ard cover on a black back beats one complete.

But Uncle Tom was allus a gurt man to 'av ev'rything proper an' vitty.

It ended:

Bless my 'eart I was agwine tew tell 'ee about our vus' meeting, but I've bide yer tellin' and tellin' 'bout wan thing an' t'other—never min', I'll write 'ee anither letter 'um by,

Very respectably,
JAN STEWER

Coles later estimated Jan's age to be permanently sixty-five; he gave it as fifty-seven in 'Jan and the Census Paper', the best of the monologues. Characteristically, Jan mixes it up with 'total chillern born alive'; 'Must a-bin while I was out', drily comments Ann, his wife. Once he does indeed speak of himself as having been nineteen or twenty: 'Jis the age', he says 'when every young chap gets some fulish idaya into his head. With zome 'tis valling in love with a maid and writing love-letters up in tallet, and brushing their hair twice a day. Others goes in fer making out pautry, and some takes up local praiching. But with me 'twas the viddle.' That figures, to use a phrase that would be quite incomprehensible to Jan. It is quite in keeping with his nature that, rushing in where angels fear to tread, he should undertake some enterprise for which he is entirely unfitted.

So, as decade follows decade and as war follows war, as the Victorian age gradually approaches the permissive age, Jan remains unchanging, indestructible, immortal, commenting on the passing show, sometimes with marked asperity but always to the huge delight of his readers. Coles was greatly to develop his style of dialect-writing over the years so as to make it more easily readable, though no one, least of all he himself, then realised for how many years he was to continue 'tellin' and tellin' 'bout wan thing an' t'other'.

TWO

The Growth of Jan Stewer

Mr Gratwicke must have been a man of great discernment. In Coles's first offering to the *Devon and Exeter Gazette* there was little to suggest to the average reader the sheer brilliance of what was to follow.

The young schoolmaster went on with his teaching. One day he received a letter from Mr Gratwicke asking him to write another, similar story. He did so at irregular intervals, and gradually the now-familiar village of Muddlecombe and its inhabitants came to life. Roughly speaking, Muddlecombe was Puddington. None of Jan's fellow villagers are based on any one person: as in most fiction, each character is an amalgam of several people, and yet each one is utterly believable and real. Shamelessly, like all true artists, Coles borrowed a mannerism of speech from one, an irritating habit from another, stole one man's clothes and another's occupation—and produced Ned Annaferd. Tom Zalter is more true to life than your next-door neighbour; Lias Buzzacott is all the lovable rogues you have ever met, rolled into one; Sophy Grinnaway is every gossip you have ever known—as the familiar phrase has it, large as life and twice as natural. Truth may be stranger than fiction, but this is the sort of fiction that is truer than truth, and even A. J. C.'s next-of-kin were unaware of the parentage of Muddlecombe's inhabitants.

Some time later he received a letter from Mr Gratwicke asking for a weekly feature at ten shillings a time. A. J. C. had already found his material wearing thin, and felt that each contribution would be his last—the challenge was frightening. But it was also irresistible, for ten shillings a week was thirty per cent of his income. He accepted the challenge, and embarked on what was to become something of a record in the annals of British (let alone west-country) journalism. He created, out of his own vivid imagination and acute observation of Devonshire life, whole villages and parishes, and a character who was to become a familiar name throughout the county and, to some extent, throughout the country.

Meanwhile, Puddington carried on in its customary free and easy way, totally unaware that it was harbouring a genius in the person of the likeable, spare-framed young schoolmaster. He in fact dropped quiet hints, but of a kind that would not betray his authorship. He waited to hear opinions of the paper's new feature, and it was quite in keeping with his vanity that he hoped they would not be too candid. But he got the impression that nobody had even read it: folk went about their work as usual, talked of their ploughings and tillings, their fields and their families, their pots and pans, pigs and poultry. The butcher and baker called, women hung out their washing, men strolled over to the Black Dog for their evening pint, the latest war news from South Africa was discussed.

After a somewhat shaky start, Coles settled down to produce a regular weekly feature in the *Gazette* for a period of five years, passing without a break to the *Western Weekly News*, Plymouth, where for thirty-five years a story of about 2,000 words appeared regularly. There were a few gaps during the First World War, when his contributions (for he still kept them up, though far from his country) went astray.

In his weekly contribution of 11 October 1901, Jan drew an affecting picture of the 'Devons' doomed to spend another Christmas under arms in an inhospitable land—and suggested that when housewives were preparing their Christmas puddings they should make an extra one to send to the boys at the front. The paper undertook to pack and dispatch them to South Africa to be equally divided between the two battalions: this involved a 6,000 mile sea voyage in days when there were no air lifts, followed by a long trek across the veldt. The paper pointed out that 'each pudding must be mixed with nothing but eggs and brandy or it will not keep. It must be boiled not less than three hours and must be thoroughly dried before it is sent to us.' It was recommended that the puddings be made in enamel basins, and that on the cloth covering of each the name and address of the sender should be pinned, 'with wishes for a happy Christmas'. Readers who could not manage to send puddings were invited to contribute tobacco or cash. Parcels began to arrive almost immediately and continued in a steady stream. Hampers arrived with six, eight or ten puddings; and the Mayoress of Okehampton and a ladies' committee sent sixty-eight.

All this was something of a pleasant embarrassment to the *Gazette* office staff, and space had to be found for packing the puddings into hermetically sealed cases. Altogether nearly a thousand were despatched to Southampton, and A. J. C. went to Exeter from Puddington to see them taken to the station in the horse-drawn lorry. One grateful soldier gave Jan a wooden pipe of the deep-bowled type common in South Africa, having spent several hours carving on it the arms and motto of the Transvaal. This he sent, with the knife he had, but unfortunately it was among the treasures lost in the 1942 blitz. Twenty-five years after the Boer War ended, Coles was giving a Jan Stewer recital in a large north-country town. At the end of the show a man came to the dressing-room with an extended hand. 'You don't know me,' he said, 'but in Christmas of 1901 I ate your health in South Africa in a slice of "mother's pudding". It made all the difference, and I want to shake hands with you.'

Jan's village is Muddlecombe, and it was from old friends and relatives in and around Puddington that Muddlecombe and Jan came to life. One source was an old uncle who lived a few miles from Tiverton, in a farmhouse where, in early youth, Coles had spent a holiday. Once, on his return from Tiverton market, this usually quiet little man related to his young nephew an incident which was, along with others described in the following pages, later included in many public performances:

I was gwain down over Gold Street Heel when I zee'd a feller coming up tother zide the road. I thought to mezelf, 'Caw, darn my wig, I knaws you. Now, who be you?'

I knawed the feller, zee, so well as I knaws you. But I could'n call 'en home. And I kep lookin' at 'n, and lookin' an 'n, and thinkin' 'Who be you?' And he was lookin' to me, zee, and he was thinkin' 'zac'ly the zame, I could zee he was. He was thinkin' to hiszelf, 'Caw, darn 'ee, I knaws you. Now, who be you?'

And I was lookin' to he, and he was lookin' to me, and I was thinkin' 'Who be you?' and he was thinkin' 'Who be you?' So I started to cross the road; and he started to cross the road likewise. And when us met in the middle, 'twasn't neether one of us.

Another example related by Coles was that of Farmer Williams returning home from market on his horse. Having talked business with other farmers in the Market House Inn, the Turk's Head and the Seven Stars, he left the geography of the homeward journey to his stone-cold-sober horse. Jogging along the road in a measure known as 'dree-appence an' tuppence, dree-appence an' tuppence,'—A. J. Coles later brought this to life on stage with consummate artistry—the farmer was bobbing up and down when suddenly something frightened the horse, which jumped just as William was 'up at the top of his stroke.' Picking himself up, the farmer went after the horse as well as he could until he came to a fork in the road and, not knowing which way the horse had taken, called to a man working in the hedge: 'Yer! Have you zeed'd a hoss go along yer?' 'Yes, zur. I zee'd a hoss go along just now.' 'Was there anybody on the back of 'n?' 'No, master, there wad'n nobody on the back of 'n.' 'Aw! That must have been me, then.'

Coles once told me the story of a small man with a big voice who lived in an even smaller village than his own Puddington. Most of the services in the 'Methody' chapel (which, he explained, could mean any Nonconformist denomination and not necessarily Methodist, from which it obviously derived) were conducted by laymen, which is certainly the case in Methodism today. In those days, more than is the case now, their zeal often outran their scholarship. The preacher on this occasion had a strange habit of jingling together words of a similar sound, a kind of involuntary punning of which he himself was entirely unaware. His sermons were always extempore and, he would proudly claim, delivered 'on the spurt of the moment'. In the neighbourhood was a workman named Dick Bradford who, during the winter, added to his income by an operation known as 'ripping' (felling trees and taking as his perk the bark to sell to the tan-yard). Declaimed the preacher: 'In Westbridge Wood, to cut off the branches of the hoaks and the hellums you haves the haxe of Dick Bradford; and in the Bible, to cut off the branches of hignorance and sin, you haves the haxe of the Apostles.' The same preacher never hesitated to illustrate an allusion by referring, not always in a complimentary manner, to someone known to all the congregation. Dan Parkhouse was well known as an inveterate narrator of his own personal experiences and adventures, and would often stretch the truth to make it fit the circumstances. It was this characteristic that the preacher once used to drive home his point: 'When Dan Parkhouse tells 'ee aught, you says "Pass me the salt." But when the Lord tells 'ee aught, you get the salt that have not lost its saviour.'

Coles also recalled an incident of this early period in the parish church of another remote village. Farmer William had two marked characteristics in his religious observance: a distaste of 'Methodies' as such, and a very loud singing voice. Loudness was indeed the chief virtue of his voice, for in such trifles as tune and time he followed his own humour. Where he went, the organist and the rest of the congregation had to go, or wait until he arrived; it was useless attempting another verse until he had finished the preceding one. One Sunday morning Farmer William was missing from the family pew. Conjecture ran riot among the groups lingering at the church after the service as to the cause of his absence—every conceivable reason was advanced, from indigestion to a calving cow. The village received a major shock when it learned that William Hammett had that morning attended the service in the Methody chapel. He repeated the visit the next Sunday, and declared his intention of continuing to do so; and when, more in sorrow than anger, a neighbour reproved him for deserting the church of his forefathers, he replied:

That's all well an' gude, Mr Sercombe. But 'tis like this-yer. I've attended church rig'ler as clockwork, as you do know, all the days o' my life, and should have went on doing so til I was took there in a timbern coat. But Georgie Snell had the darn cheek to tell me I was zinging too loud and playing Old Harry with the sarvice. So I said to 'en, 'Look yer, George Snell,' I says, 'when I takes a load of turmits out to the sheep, they holleys "Baa" to let me know where they be to. And when I'm to church I likes to holley "Baa" in me awn way, to let the Almighty know where I be to.'

'That's all right, Mr Hammett,' he says, 'but there's no call for 'ee to holley in the Almighty's yer-ole.'

So I've took my zinging to chapel, and there I can open my bellises and let rip.

A. J. C. knew Old Thomas, one of the village's oldest inhabitants, very well. The old man retired, and was seated, one sunny day, in front of his small cottage on a bench. The local minister, passing by, saw a golden opportunity to give him a chance of repentance as his life neared its end—Old Thomas had not adhered unwaveringly to the straight and narrow way—and sat beside him. Old Thomas listened attentively to all the statutory punishments that awaited him, and then wheezed through his denuded gums: 'No, zur; you'm wrong. You'm wrong, zur. I won't say but I might have to wail but' (with a chuckle of immense self-satisfaction) ' 'twill take 'em all their time to make me gash me teeth.' Old Thomas had been a moderately successful farmer, and was a sturdy character, but in conversation he had a habit of exaggerated civility which a stranger might well mistake for servility. He 'sir'd' everybody in every other sentence, and his replies were interlarded with 'your honour' and 'your worship'. (Coles worked the malapropism 'gash' into more than one tale, and the old man's apparent servility into 'The Swell Dinner'.) It was said that the dark patch in the front of the brim of Thomas's hat was a grease spot caused by the frequency with which he touched it when talking to strangers.

At one time a young man, unfamiliar with country ways, was spending a holiday with the local squire, to whom he was related. One day, when he condescended to stop and chat with Farmer Thomas in the village street, the old man responded with many touchings of his hat and a liberal sprinkling of 'Yes, your worship' and 'No, your honour'. 'That's all right, my good man,' said the youth with patronising affability, 'you need not keep repeating "your honour". Once now and then is quite sufficient to show respect.' Old Thomas did not turn a hair but, with another pinch of the brim of his hat and a grandfatherly smile, replied 'Don't you worry yourself about that, your worship. 'Tis only our old-fashioned items. I says "your honour" to you the same as I says "my dear" to the hoss.'

Old Thomas was not a regular churchgoer, but once he went to a harvest festival where the visiting clergyman preached at inordinate length and in a condescending manner which did nothing to endear him to his audience. The clergyman stayed the night at the rectory, and the next morning walked down a lane to catch the carrier's cart at the turnpike. On the way he passed one of Thomas's fields, where the old fellow was at work just inside the gate. Having plenty of time on hand, the parson stopped to talk. 'You know, my friend,' he said, 'you English farmers should be more up to date and adopt modern methods. Otherwise you will be left all behind. Do you know, I could buy better wheat all the way from America for fifteen shillings than you could grow for a pound.' 'I darezay you could, zur', replied Thomas quite placidly. 'And do you know, your honour, I could buy a better sarment for tuppence than you could preach in a month o' Sundays.'

One day a party of visitors arrived in the village square. One elderly gentleman, speaking in a broad Scots accent and pointing to the church, said to an old resident, 'I beg your parrdon my frriend, could you inforrm me, is there any early Norrman architecture in the toor of yon kirk?' 'Zammy,' called the man to a fellow villager, 'have 'ee got your watch? There's a French chap yer wants to know the time.'

In Puddington, A. J. C. spent much of his spare time in the workshop of Ned Knowles, the village wheelwright and carpenter, where he was initiated into the secrets of the craft. Using Ned's primitive lathe he turned out quantities of legs for stools and made picture frames, a skill he later admitted he had never mastered. But after an hour in Ned's company, as he worked and talked at his bench, an instalment for next week's issue would begin to take shape. There was no pub in the parish, so Ned's workshop became a natural meeting-place for villagers to discuss the affairs of both the neighbourhood and the great world beyond, with an untutored originality and a native wit that were a source of delight. Many of Ned's expressions unconsciously added to the evolving character of Jan Stewer.

The villagers' geography of the world, said Coles, comprised six majordivisions: Devon, London, tother side o' London, up-the-country, furrin' parts, and Cornwall. Every personage and happening could be assigned to one or other of those areas; any that could not definitely be ascribed to either of the first five went into the sixth. During the early stages of the Boer War, the Boxer trouble came to a head in China, and in the summer of 1900 a British punitive force was sent to Peking. One morning, while the papers were full of the new trouble in the Far East, A. J. C. met old Robert: 'Poor old Buller will have enough to do now, with these-yer Boxers joining in,' said Robert. 'Oh,' said Coles, 'the Boxers are fighting in China.' 'Yes, I know,' came the reply, 'but it's all out around that district.' When reports came through of a considerable retreat, A. J. C. expected to find his friend jubilant, and said to him 'Good news this morning, Robert.' 'It's all right, in a way, I suppose. The only thing I don't like is, the further they Boers retreats back, the nearer they gets to we.' And, as Eric Morecambe would say, there's no answer to that.

Ned Knowles was a craftsman who took such a pride in his workmanship that he never made much money—a type fast disappearing. On one occasion, the parish squire ordered a wagonette from a reputable firm of carriage-builders in another part of the country. He was a fastidious man, but he approved of the vehicle when it arrived, except for the wheels which he considered too heavy-looking for the lines of the body. The makers assured him anything less robust would not stand up to the bumps and jolts of rough roads and lanes. One day the squire, passing through Puddington, asked Ned his opinion. This, said Ned, was 'a butiful bit of bodywork, sure nuff'. 'What about the wheels, Ned?' 'Aw, they wheels will take 'ee anywhere, Squire. They'll never let 'ee down.' 'I don't suppose they will—but what do you think of the look of 'em?' 'Plenty strong enough for the job I should think, zur.' 'I say they're too heavy-looking.' 'I was just gwain to zay the zame thing, zur. I think they'm hugly big, if you ask me.' 'The makers say if they were any lighter they wouldn't be safe for my work.' This touched Ned on a sensitive spot. He always 'reckoned he could make a wheel, if naught else'. 'I could make 'ee lighter wheels than that, maister.' 'To stand up to the job?' 'If they don't I'll make 'ee another for naught.'

Ned turned out the wheels with all the skill and loving care he had. They were so much slimmer that even the squire felt a little doubtful on first seeing them. 'They look very nice, Ned, but don't you think they're a trifle too delicate for this country?' 'You know what I told 'ee, zur, daun' 'ee?' Some time later A. J. C. was walking with Ned in Fore Street, Tiverton. A smart wagonette, drawn by a pair of fine horses and driven by the squire himself, came along the street. As soon as he saw it, the little carpenter stopped short and gripped A. J. C. by the arm. 'I made they wheels, maister, I made they wheels,' he said excitedly. 'I made they wheels, I made they wheels, maister.' He repeated this in a crescendo as the vehicle approached, even louder and more quickly as it passed, and in *diminuendo rallentando* as it gradually disappeared. When it had gone from sight, he turned and assured his companion again, 'I made they wheels.'

Once Coles persuaded Ned to drive him in his trap, pulled by a sturdy Dartmoor pony, to visit some relatives. This was the longest journey 'abroad' the little wheelwright had taken up to then; and after driving for some hours through the countryside he observed gravely, almost with awe, 'Isn't it amazing? No matter where you go, somebody lives there.'

Other journeys that brought A. J. C. pleasure and profit were the frequent rides in the carrier's cart (later immortalised in *In a Devonshire Carrier's Van*). His fellow passengers, on their way to market, gossiped constantly and perhaps not always charitably, though for the most part the humour was of the leg-pulling type. There was an easy-going atmosphere in that unsophisticated countryside in the pre-war years: no one yet knew how many villages were to be denuded of their young men. Coles entered wholeheartedly into the spirit of these journeys and meanwhile, sometimes consciously, sometimes unconsciously, he was building up from the rich rustic characters around him the villages of Muddlecombe, Barleycombe, Raxun and Week St Agnes. (Muddlecombe and neighbouring Barleycombe evinced a friendly rivalry towards each other: Muddlecombe always liked to be 'upzides with they to Barleycombe'.) Jan Stewer was becoming a familiar name, and his personality was developing and becoming fully rounded. In the carrier's cart, in the Black Dog, in the settle of the chimney corner, many a yarn was told that would be the inspiration of what was soon known as 'Jan's old logic'.

In 1913 Coles and his wife moved to Torquay. He was now a family man, with two sons and two daughters. The boys, the senior half of the quartet, were going to Newton Abbot Grammar School, the elder girl was going to a kindergarten, and the younger one would be three next birthday. Their father was elected to the borough council as a member for the Torre Ward. The dialect stories continued, and did not cease when the First World War was declared. When this occurred Coles was thirty-eight, but he was also patriotic and keen to join up. He had had some military experience, having enlisted in the Artillery in 1892 and been stationed in Dover Castle. In 1914 he went to several recruiting stations, only to be told each time that he was too old. But early in 1915 an urgent order was issued by the War Office that men with previous experience in the Artillery should be enlisted regardless of the age limit. Coles just came into this category, and wrote to the War Office pointing out the fact. A telegram came back, to the effect that 'this man is to be enlisted if willing and fit', which he carried to a senior friend in Exeter. This friend suggested that Coles come to his place for the medical examination rather than stand around in a queue in a blanket. A. J. C. was fearful that the fact that he could not read without glasses might fail him and so, having been shown into a hut where he was left alone for nearly half an hour, he committed to memory the sight chart hanging behind the door. Later, when asked to read the chart, he started with the big letters and then continued to recite from memory. Suddenly he became aware of a movement by the doctor and realised he had begun to read newspaper type at ten feet. His dramatic instinct came to his aid: making a half-step forward and screwing up his eyes, he said, 'I'm afraid I can't read any more, sir.' 'I shouldn't damn well think you could. Extraordinary sight.'

In 1917, he was in charge of the pay office at Mustapha Camp, a few miles from Alexandria. The air was hot and heavy, and the conditions were arduous. Work was always at full pressure, because this was not a battalion or recognised unit but a 'common Depot'—a sort of human dump, with troops constantly arriving at short notice, comprising the odds and ends of almost every branch of the army, mostly discharged from hospitals. The soldiers would stay at Mustapha until fit—possibly for a matter of days—after which they would leave for their units and their places be taken by others. They came from every front—France, Italy, Salonika, Palestine, Mesopotamia. It was no joke examining thousands of paybooks which had been entered up in francs, liras, piastres or rupees. Careful examination was essential: figures were sometimes manipulated so that an actual debit was turned to an apparent credit; and it was not unknown for a man to hand in as his own the paybook of a dead comrade whose account was on the right side. It was sometimes difficult to tell exactly which unit a man belonged to, as transferences were constantly taking place. The payroll amounted to thousands of pounds a week, and since a slip might involve the commanding officer in a serious personal loss, it was an anxious and at times nerve-wracking job.

On one occasion, just as the staff was hoping to knock off for the Saturday afternoon, a party of new arrivals was announced. The voice of the orderly sergeant came up from the parade ground as he checked the 'nominal roll': 'Party—'chun!'

'One.' 'Two.' 'Three.' '*Vower.*' 'Five.' 'Six.' A. J. C. turned to the orderly and said, 'When the party is dismissed, send up Number Four of the front rank.' The man came in, shaken by malaria and clearly a stone or two below his normal weight. But A. J.C. recognised him. 'What's your name?' he asked. 'Private Rice, zur.' 'Where do you come from?' 'Mesopotamia.' 'No, no, I don't mean now. Before you joined up.' 'Nuton Abbot, zur.' 'Ever seen me before?' 'No, zur.' 'Take another look.' The man looked at him more closely, his stiffened posture sagged and became most unmilitary. 'Aw, mai gude lor, if 'tid'n Mr Coles.' Twelve clerks burst out laughing, then pretended they were only coughing. But soon everyone was laughing—a sound that was to become increasingly familiar to Jan Stewer in a few years.

Prior to this, while Coles was still a corporal, he was treated in hospital for a gastric ulcer when in Gosport, which kept him from being sent to France. Much to his annoyance he had an 'office' job, and was to be sent to the Isle of Wight for convalescence. By this time he weighed less than seven stone, and, while waiting in line for a last inspection, he fainted from weakness. His temperature was taken, and he was rushed back to bed in the same hospital. His delirious state coincided with the day of the week on which for many years he had posted his 'copy'—usually he left it to the last moment, for he was by nature a great procrastinator. Something must have told his deranged reason that the critical moment had arrived, and he called frantically for writing materials. The hospital staff tried to pacify him, but he insisted that his contribution must be written and dispatched at once or it would be too late. At last, in desperation, they gave him a sheet of paper supported on his diet-board, and a pencil. He wrote for an hour, feverishly, without a pause. Or rather, he scrawled long strings of utterly unintelligible hieroglyphics—across the sheet, diagonally, lines over lines, criss-cross, sometimes on the paper, sometimes on the diet-board—all at full speed. When the scrawl reached the foot of the page it went back to the top, and the next part was scribbled over the previous absurdity. The poor nurse was in tears, but when at last he broke off exhausted, she pretended to place the manuscript in an envelope and take it to the post. Then, satisfied, Coles fell asleep.

Within two days a telegram reached his wife in Torquay saying, 'Husband dangerously ill suffering from pneumonia.' There was no telephone in the house in those days, so his nine-year-old daughter Mary was rushed off to Torre Station to find out train times so that Florence could leave at once. She arrived at the hospital in time for what everyone thought was his last gasp; oxygen was being used to keep him alive until she arrived. But he pulled through, and with some string-pulling got himself sent to Egypt, where he collapsed again after only a short time. However, those two years in the sun cured all his ills, including the neuritis which had plagued him for years. He always said it was the Egyptian sun which had made a new man of him. He entertained troops by the thousand, and was a godsend to war-weary men resting after a spell of combat. Wherever he travelled—Cairo, Port Said, Alexandria, Tasmalia—he took with him his one-string fiddle made out of a cigar box, and his ventriloquist's doll, Old Peter. In the pay office, he began as a private and became a bombardier (the equivalent of a sergeant today). He once succeeded in getting to the French coast, but because of his health he was put on the next boat back. While in Egypt he learnt a little Arabic and, on receiving his commission was put in command of the Egyptian labour corps. These were the days when petrol came in two-gallon cans and had to be taken from the holds of ships. With characteristic contrivance, Coles encouraged the workers to work in time to their native rhythms, and discovered that 'as long as they sang, they could do anything'.

Once, while at the base at Alexandria where he was sent after his breakdown in health, he found himself back in a previous camp at Gabari—the only soul in about thirty empty tents. The next evening he

3. Trio from 'Jan's Concert Party'.
   L to R: Colin, Harry and A. J. Coles.

4. Poster from the London production of *Barnet's Folly*, 1935.

wandered through the streets of Alexandria, feeling unwell and utterly wretched, and unwittingly found himself in a long queue of soldiers outside the Alhambra where free concerts for the 'Tommies' were given every Sunday evening. He drifted in with the stream, and listened to a series of items that did nothing to allay his gloom. And then he heard a rough, homely voice come rolling in from the stage in the richest of dialect: 'Ladies and gentlemen, I am going to tell you how an old-fashioned Devonshire farmer went for the first time in his life to a swell dinner.' He sat up as if electrified, as one of Jan's stories came floating through the theatre. On the stage was his old friend Charles Balchin of Exeter, who told the anecdote so well that the vast house was soon filled with laughter. The only person not laughing was A. J. Coles; there was a lump in his throat, and he was glad it was dark.

He was demobolised in the autumn of 1919, and returned to Torquay. On his arrival one morning he was caught in a snow shower, and he started to cross Fleet Street to shelter in the post office when, half-way across, he became vaguely conscious of an absence of movement and sound. Even two approaching cars were stopped, their engines hushed. Fortunately he suddenly realised what was happening, in time to save him from making a *faux pas*—for he was still in uniform, and it would have looked bad for a British officer to be striding obliviously through the first observance of the two minutes' silence. He remained in the middle of the road, still alone; yet not alone, for he was striving with a mind suddenly crowded with a jostling host of memories too recent for comfort.

THREE

From a Carrier's Van

A. J. Coles once told me he had met a man who professed to have read everything Coles had ever written. This astounding claim, could it ever be substantiated, would certainly deserve a place in the *Guinness Book of Records*, for Coles's output was enormous. Every week for over half a century Jan Stewer's dialect writings were eagerly awaited, not only in Devon but also in many a Cornish or Somerset home. Indeed, his fame had spread even further afield, and it is not too much to say that enthusiastic readers of his work were to be found in all parts of the country and several parts of the world. It was, for many, the high spot of the week.

Letters began pouring into the newspaper office from Africa, China, Peru and isolated spots in the dominions. One arrived safely from a 'one hoss' town (the description was the correspondent's) far out in the north-west territory some hundred miles or so from Calgary, Alberta: it was addressed to 'Jan Stewer, England.' Another was from a Devonian in South America, working in a remote spot miles from the nearest Englishman. His monthly mail included, he wrote,

four welcome instalments of Jan Stewer, and on a few occasions even five. What these bits of the old tongue mean to me you cannot imagine. I keep out one copy to read and lock the remainder in the safe, religiously rationing myself to one a week. The temptation is to read them all right off, but then I would have no Jan Stewer to look forward to for three or four weeks. So I force myself to keep the rules.

Some of the tales were uproariously funny, others were just straightforward narratives, but all showed the writer's keen psychological insight into the vagaries of human nature. It is not to be wondered at that Coles was sometimes stuck for an idea, upon which, at times, he would turn to his son Harry and say, 'I've dried up. I don't know what to write about next.' And Harry would say, 'What about someone raising and then losing a prime turkey?' 'Fine!' his father would reply, 'that'll keep me going for six weeks.' And thus another serialised tale would eventually find its way into print.

Could one read them all, it would be like browsing through the bound volumes of old copies of *Punch*, for they provide a fascinating sociological study of English life from the Boer War right up to the years following the Second World War. Two examples illustrate this point. One is the story called 'The 'Orrible Skirt'—at least, so Mrs Snell called it, but Jan corrected her: ' 'Obble skirts, you manes missis,' I says, ' 'Obble, not 'orrible'.' When Georgie Coomes saw a woman coming out of Muddlecombe church wearing a hobble skirt, he called out 'Look, soce, 'tis a sack raace.' 'The 'Orrible Skirt' is certainly a period piece if ever there was one, but still makes delightful reading, with its description of their wearers' attempts to negotiate 'the stile there by Varmer Blake's cottage. Tid'n the best o' stiles to get ovver in any cloas, but in 'orrible skirts I'm beggared if 'tid'n a master-piece.' The second example, culled from the *Western Weekly News* of 3 May 1937, is a colourful description of 'tettyvatin Muddlecombe for the Coronation'. Dancing around the maypole was only part of the proceedings, which ended with everyone seated in the Institute or the square listening to the King's broadcast message to his people. ' 'Twill be the fust time they've bin quiet for the day; and the women-volk will say out, what the men be thinking to theirsel's—"Bless the dear heart of 'en, and the Quane, and they two swit li'l maidens. God bless 'em all. God zave the King." '

Week after week the stories flowed and the characters developed. Only two comparable writers immediately occur to me, in terms of continuous narratives about one location and one set of people. The first is Frank Richards with his stories of Greyfriars, the magnificent Billy Bunter dominating the school scene, that now strike a nostalgic chord in the breasts of middle-aged and elderly gentlemen. The difference is that Muddlecombe bears a stronger likeness to the typical Devonshire village than Greyfriars (or the schools that Richards created with equal profusion under other pen-names) does or ever did to the average public school. The other writer is Richmal Crompton, with her William Brown stories. Here too, village life is clearly delineated, but not that of a Devon village. The picture drawn by Crompton is just as authentic, but deals with more genteel characters: vicars' wives, commuting businessmen, mildly eccentric spinsters, John Betjeman's 'tweed-skirted females, cycling to early Communion'. Billy Bunter, William Brown and Jan Stewer have it in common that they live in closely knit communities, and that they and their associates never grow any older. They are like Dorian Gray without that tell-tale picture; the English scene changes, but they remain the same age. But for sheer staying-power, Jan surpasses the other two.

Those stories from Coles's vast output which appeared only in newspapers and were not reprinted are now available (because of space restrictions) only on microfilm. Happily, not a few found their way into book form. The first bound volume was called *Jan Stewer's Demshur Buke*, which appeared in about 1902. It was a modest little affair, wire-stretched and bound in a paper cover, and sold at a shilling. But when it appeared he was almost inordinately proud of it, and for a long time carried a copy in his pocket wherever he went. He could always be trusted to find some pretext for dragging it into the conversation, or to engineer an excuse and produce it as if he happened to have it with him by the merest chance. This book contained a few monologues which had already appeared in the *Devon and Exeter Gazette*, some of which are still firm favourites. They include the story of Jan's first and last cricket match, the episode of the Stewers' acquisition of a hot-water bottle, and 'The Hunt Dinner' (later renamed 'The Swell Dinner'). These are still recited at dinners, church or chapel guilds and the like, and never fail to bring the house down—unless they are completely murdered, as is sometimes the case. Yet however poor the performance, their intrinsic wit atones to some degree. Many do them well, though even the proudest performer would not compare his or her renderings with those of their creator.

Less rare than the *Demshur Book* and *Jan Stewer at Home and Abroad* are the series *In a Devonshire Carrier's Van*, produced in what would today be called paperbacks. They are, in a sense, embryos of the more polished versions later published by Herbert Jenkins. These 'Tales told in the Devon Dialect', as they were sub-titled, also sold at a shilling each. 'Reuben Ley in the Higher Circle', not reprinted in the hardback editions, is an example of the countryman's sense of unease when one of his children marries into another class. On this occasion, he was thereby drawn into the complications of a garden party. It begins: 'Reuben Ley was sot back in the back part o' the van. He was zo quiet us didn' 'ardly nawtice 'en fer a bit—dimpsey and all.' This is the environment common to all the tales. One copy has a delightful frontispiece, a photograph captioned 'On the Road to Market—Another Passenger'. This shows the carrier's cart, pulled by two sturdy horses and already containing three contemporary rustic passengers, temporarily stopped to take in a fourth party, a woman with two shopping baskets in her hands and wearing a voluminous long black skirt. One regrets the lack of publication dates in these books, but they were certainly pre-1914. This is clear not only from the prices in the advertisements inside the back and front covers ('real silver watches for twenty shillings'), but also from the delightful naïvety of the rustics lovingly delineated by Coles, which has since long been replaced by a sophistication as inevitable as it is regrettable. An unconsciously humorous item in one of these books is a genuine advertisement. It reads:

BIBBING'S BURDOCK PILLS
40 Years Before the Public.

The best HERBAL, PURIFYING MEDICINE ever compounded for old or young, composed of Burdock, Dandelion, Chamomile, Podophyllin, and the finest Turkey Rhubarb, contained with other gentle vegetable aperients. They cleanse the Blood from all impurities, give strength and tone to the stomach and digestive organs, and health and energy to the whole system. A marvellous remedy for Eczema, Pimples, Blackheads, Erysipelas, Bad Legs, and all skin diseases. A ready relief for Headache, Bile, Wind, Spasms, and Constipation. A positive cure for Jaundice and Liver Complaint, Indigestion and Influenza. Their cleansing and solvent action prevents the formation of stone in kidneys or bladder, and eradicates gall-stones and gravel by carrying off the poisonous uric acid. A most valuable medicine for ladies (especially for change of life), being gently purgative with marvellous searching and purifying properties. When other remedies fail, try Bibbing's Burdock Pills. Don't wait—start now. The first dose will convince any sufferer who wishes to FEEL well, LOOK well, and KEEP well. Sold in boxes at 1/1½ and 2/9, or post free from J. H. Bibbings, Pharmacist, Burdock Pill Factory, Newton Abbot.

In 'Pity the Poor Foreigner', Mrs Endycott speaks of her attempts to make herself understood by 'furriners' who were 'stappin' durin' the zummer months . . . They'd a-got wrong names for ev'ry blessid thing.' The foreign lady eventually succeeded in making it clear that she wanted to know how much butter was:

' "Shullnapmy [one shilling and a halfpenny] a pound," I zes, zac'ly like that. Plains cude be. An' do you knaw, that wumman med me raypate it twenty times if her did wonce.
"How much?" her goes again.
"Shullnapmy a pound," I zes, quite as plain as that. "Shullnapmy a pound." '

She quotes the Bible to support her contention that names (English names, of course) were 'first gived out in the Garden of Eden . . . So it can't be right fer thase yer furriners to go caalin' things what they was never intended.' Confronted with the argument that there is biblical authority for the Tower of Babel being the cause of diverse languages, she is only momentarily confounded.

'I knaws all 'bout that,' zes Missis Endycott; 'But that daun' alter it in the laistest degree. I knaws they caaled things wrong names fer a bit, but 'ow long did it last? Can you show me any place in the Baible arter that where a 'oss is caaled aught else but a 'oss, or a shool aught else but a shool.'
'Naw,' sez Tom. 'I dunnaw as I can.'
'Very well, then,' sez missis.

These tales have a distinctive period flavour all their own. There is a school of thought which in fact holds that the original series, as opposed to the revised version published by Herbert Jenkins, is more authentic. The stories from it are still used for public recitations and readings, in preference to what some people consider to be the over-sophistication of the later editions. This is not a point of view to which I adhere, although it must be admitted that the early tales contain much that never found its way into the later books and are much to be treasured on that account. Much of the dialect is stronger than in Coles's later writings, where it was toned down to make the works palatable for the many non-west-country readers who were beginning to read the inimitable Jan Stewer. Asides such as the following did not make for easy reading aloud in public: 'Come up, Damzel-ah; Prince-ah; wug-aff. Way-ya! Jim jump an' putt on the drug--right—Damzel-ah! Kimm-up 'oss! Kim-eer—'way. Yu maaze toad—wat's matter with 'ee?'

Only a person with a keen ear could have reproduced these invocations so exactly. Coles, in fact, later polished up some of the more obvious pieces for public recitation, but there is a homeliness about the originals which captures precisely the cosy atmosphere of those leisurely days. Even then, Tom Zalter was philosophising:

Things bant no more like they use to be than a arple's like a nit. There! I doan spose us kin expec' that they shude be; but saame time it du sim a pity like to think wat a lot o' the 'ole customs be passin' away, arter they bin orwiz the rules vir hunderds o' years as the sayin' is.

There is an authenticity rarely attained by Devonshire writers in the story 'The Man Who Never Told a Lie', as regards both the perfectly rendered vowel sounds and the general atmosphere. This is, to all appearances, the first tale in the initial *Carrier's Van* series, and it introduces one of the village's best-known and much-quoted characters, Tom Zalter. It is he who drives the carrier's cart to Exeter every Friday (market day). It begins: 'When a man tells 'ee that he nivver told a lai in his life,' says Mr Zalter, 'yu'm quite safe in bettin' a hogshaid o' zider to a 'ap'ney caake that he's utherways jis told 'ee wan, or else there's wan coming now purty quick. And a middlin' gude size wan, too.' And it ends: 'Wull, yer us be, all change vir Muddlecombe. Come on, Missis Porter. I doan winder yu carn get up very aisy, I be darned if yu ant upssut Missis Cann's pot of traicle, an' now yule be abble to hire yerself out so much a-nour as a walking fly paper.' The story describes in minute detail the weekly ritual of piling up customers' belongings and (on the return journey) purchases. ' 'Coorse, I carls'n Maister Zalter to yu out of perliteness like,' Jan explains. And then, with the Devonians' own staggering logic, he adds, 'Ezekiel Zalter's name is and so 'e orwis goes by the naame o' Tom.'

'The Best Lies Deepest', one of Coles's little romantic tales which only just stop short this side of sentimentality, is perhaps of most interest now because of this piece of dialogue at the outset:

'Have 'e yerd the latest news, Jan?' says Miss's Snell.
'Dunnaw,' I says. 'How long have it bin out? I've yerd that Varmer Long los' a bullik las' Tuesday wik, an' I've yerd that Sarah James weared her las' zummer's hat to church las' Zindy, trimmed up to make 'en 'pear like a new wan. Is ther' ought later'n that?'
'Have 'e yerd that Dick Bradley got a baaby?'
'No,' I says, 'I ad'n yerd that.'
'Wull, he hath, then,' her says.
'Hath-a? That's cont'ry to what folks expected id'n it?' I says.
'Wull, he's wive have,' her says.
'Wat is it?' says Tom, 'boy or cheel?'
' 'Tis a boy,' says missis. 'Brave, fine cheel, they say. I ant zeed 'en, not 'eet.'

In this context, 'cheel' means first 'girl' and then, more understandably, in the second instance 'child'. Coles used to explain that the query 'Wat is it—boy or cheel?' was not a feeble stock joke, but was simply being Anglo-Saxon. He pointed out that the word 'cheel' did not appear in English until somewhere about the thirteenth century, and he believed it only occurred twice in the Bible. In those days 'child' obviously stood for 'girl'. Coles illustrated the point by saying that even Shakespeare used the phrase: the old shepherd in *The Winter's Tale*, on finding the baby, says, 'Mercy on's, a bairn; a very pretty bairn. A boy or a child, I wonder?'

The above passage is also interesting for its use of the biblical 'hath'. My maternal grandfather, a broad-speaking Devonian, peppered his speech with 'hath', 'doth' and 'saith', sadly heard little, if ever, today; his whole outlook on life and his way of talking was entirely in line with that of Jan in the *Carrier's Van* tales. He used to tell me how the inhabitants of the village in which he lived were warned by an American that the world was coming to an end on a specific day. As a consequence, none of them troubled to buy any more coal or groceries than would last beyond that date; for, with what seems to us today to be astonishing naïvety, they assumed that the prophecy must be true because it was told to them by an American. The story, which he told me many times when I was a little boy and which never varied by a single syllable, ended: 'And then the day come when 'twas spaused to be the end of the world. And us waited. And us waited. And then us knawed 'twad'n true, 'cus there us was.'

The two men never met; but it was from such characters as my mother's father—one of whose expressions was 'What they will make fer money, as the woman zed when 'er zee'd the monkey'—that Coles fashioned his tales. William Littlejohns, as was his name, was pure *Carrier's Van* material, and living proof to me that the speech and idiom of the Muddlecombians of those early tales were utterly authentic.

A little strained, but delightful in its ingenuity, is Jan's interpretation of 'L'Entente Municipale' in the newspaper, in days when the phrase was being fashioned.

'Wull,' I says, 'jidgin be the shaape o't, I shid zay tiz Vrainch. Lets tare'n abroad a bit, an' vine the meanin' o't. Thur's a HAM (M), and a YEW (U), an' a HANE (N), to the vore aind, and that's MOON vir certin; an' ther's a PAI (P), an' a HAY (A), an' a HUL (L), an' a HEE (E) to the tail aind; an' that's PALE, idn' it? meanin' to zay 'twas all pale an' white in the moonshine. Wull 'n, in the middle ther's HI (I), an' a SEE (C), an' a HI (I), an' that's ICY. So I shid zay 'tis meanin', 'TWAS VULL MOON AN' DOOSTED COLD.'

In the *Carrier's Van* tales there is a glimpse of the villagers' and Jan's contempt for what, not long before, were referred to as 'horseless carriages'. Jan's adventures in his own car, Ole Biskit, lay ahead, and Tom Zalter would later succumb to progress and drive a bus; but meanwhile we are still reading excerpts like 'Tom 'anged up the reins to the hook in the tap o' the van, an' let th' osses goo 'long be therzel's'. And when a car goes rushing by—at all of thirty miles an hour, no doubt—he exclaims 'Darn they blimmin' ole things. I weesh th' Ole Nick 'ud vly away wi' ev'ry wan a'm, and they wat draives min too.' And to the horse he says, 'Damzel-ah! stan' still mumpaid. Ee's goo now my buty; although 'eev lef' a purty gude stinch be'ind en vir us to remember'n by.' There also followed the hilarious tale of 'The Jibbing Moter':

'Chap's oss 'ave jibbed,' says Bill Spriggs, 'I shid put the whip about en if I was 'e, eh Jimmy?'
'Ees begad,' says Jimmy.
'Idden thur nobody belongin' to'n?' Jan axed Tom Mudvird.
'Ess,' says Tom, 'ther' e is lookee. Cass'n zee the vit o'n sticked out be'ind. E've gone in to vinish sayin' 'ees prayers which us disturbed 'n in the middle o'.'
'Vunny sort o' prayers what I yerd,' says 'Arry Gurnslade.

This is less easy reading, for the uninitiated, than the later writings, but read aloud by a Devonian it sounds exactly right. It is the true, hard dialect magnificently translated into print, and no one ever came within a mile of Coles at this game. It was part of his skill that he later maintained (except for the ultra-purists) the authentic dialect in a simpler, more readable form. He evolved his own expression of the idiom, and would never misspell for the sake of it. He represented the Devon tongue, and the tone of the villagers, as truly as the better-known Eden Phillpotts. The older writer was meanwhile encouraging the rising talent, and the following appeared in one of the *Carrier's Van* books:

Jan Stewer and
Mr Eden Phillpotts

Jan Stewer once sent a Christmas card to Phillpotts, which took the form of a photograph of Jan and his family. In reply he received the following poem:

> TO OL' JAN STEWER AN' ·VAM'LY.
> Dear Jan, I be beholden to 'ee,
> And feel a proper joy to view 'ee
> A-sitting with your purty misses
> And they four happy little blisses.
> I never seed a braver party,
> And all so lively and so hearty.
> I send your dinky, flaxen miss,
> If she'll accept, a hugeous kiss.
> And please to give my love to t'others—
> The tibby lamb and both the brothers.
> For you and for your lady dear
> A bountiful and glad New Year.
> 'Tis Eden Phillpotts sends this rhyme,
> And hopes he'll meet 'ee some fine time.

The two writers did finally meet, although Mary, the 'dinky, flaxen miss', was forty years older before she was introduced to Phillpotts. She recalled to me going out with her father to a Women's Institute function at Broadclyst (where Phillpotts lived) just outside Exeter for a Jan Stewer evening. But just how often the two Devonshire writers met is not known.

Before passing on, let us listen again to that early voice from the days before the First World War. Jan's evocative tale of 'Boxing-Day at Muddlecombe' begins:

'Plaize to move up your zide a bit, Jim,' says Tom Zalter, the draiver, 'and make room vir Missis Grant yer. Zit up tap o' thik bag lookee; you can't 'urt nort, 'tis only zalt. Now then missis, yu squaise up tight an' carr yer basket to yer lap. That's more like Linnon. Yu zit tuther zide, Jan, an' let Missis Endycott zit 'pin your knee 'genst us comes to Lansey's Crass. Now there's rume vir yu, Missis Grant. Naw, yu baint puttin' nobody out o' the way in the laistest bit. Us be orwiz willin' to oblige the ladies, splesh'ly when they'm gude lookin'. Up yer get—I'll 'and 'ee up yer arrants. Dalled if I dawn bleeve yu gets younger ev'ry day, I du sure. Now, be all right all o' ee? You'll kip rare an' warm in there that's wan thing, you'm packed up middlin' tight together. Nivver mine, twul give 'ee better chance to tull awver wat you be gwain to give me vir a Kursmas box. On'y be carevul yu dawn' make anythin' too expensive, cuz I shid veel so baishvul 'bout exceptin' o't. Be 'e all viddy? Stiddy my deear! Dawnee start off so rash er else you want last out till us gets 'oam.'

FOUR

From Page to Stage

It has often been said that the subject of this biography had a dual personality—his own and that of his creation, Jan Stewer. The truth is less simple than that, for not only was A. J. Coles a most complex character, but even Jan Stewer has two faces.

The first of these is the Jan of the books. This Jan is far from being a merely comic character, and the same is true of the other characters so skilfully portrayed by Coles. Jan himself is an efficient and conscientious working farmer, a churchgoer, rightfully popular in Muddlecombe. He is happily married to Ann, who has a sharpish tongue at times, and a feminine contempt for the mere male's failure to comprehend the need for such annual rituals as spring-cleaning. But their mutual affection, never explicitly expressed, is quite apparent, even when they are criticising each other's foibles. Jan is conservative in outlook and distrustful of change, inclined to oppose 'newfangled inventions'. Yet hand in hand with this innate conservatism goes an incorrigible curiosity about the new and untried. Although a shrewd judge of human nature, and able to bring to life a person's essential characteristics with a vivid phrase, he is too easily persuaded against his better judgment. So he lands himself in all manner of scrapes, and engages in enterprises for which nature never intended him. On one occasion, for example, he goes to London on some unspecified errand and becomes bewildered and lost in a world of escalators, revolving doors and head-waiters. At other times he plays cricket, golf and football, rides in an aeroplane, and suffers unspeakable indignities by allowing himself to be made up as ' 'Enry Eight for a Bal Masque'. There is no end to his adventures.

Jan is not, however, just a type or merely the butt of other peoples' practical jokes; he is a distinct and likeable personality in his own right. Both he and his fellow villagers are flesh-and-blood people who never speak or act out of character: Jan would never talk in the precise idiom of Jim Davey, nor Mrs Snell in that of Sophy Grinnaway.

These are real individuals who live in a specific geographical location in Devonshire, clearly marked on the best maps.

Literalists tell me that this is not so, that Jan, his friends, and Muddlecombe itself, are all the figments of A. J. Coles's vivid imagination. As far as I am concerned this is nonsense, for Jan Stewer is now so firmly entrenched as one of this country's immortals that it is a little difficult to believe that his is only a fictional existence. G. K. Chesterton has said of Mr Pickwick that we know that if we take the high road of adventure in any acre of England we may come suddenly upon him in a lane. One has the same irrational feeling about Jan Stewer, and I have always half expected to meet him one day on my Devonshire travels, near one of the old-style wooden mileposts pointing to Muddlecombe in one direction and Barleycombe in another.

Jan is both conservative and adventurous: no carpenter, he tries his hand at building a shed; undomesticated, he has a go at paper-hanging. After each fresh initiation into the unknown, he points to the moral: leave well alone, know your limitations, don't try to ape the 'bettermos' volk'; and he is full of regrets and self-reproach ('I'd no business bein' there 'tall. If I'd bide home about me work 'twude never have happened.'). A week passes, and his insatiable curiosity or good nature (for he is too easily persuaded against his better judgment) gets the better of him; and, nothing daunted, he continues to grapple with the malevolence of inanimate objects.

There is a good deal of A. J. Coles in this Jan, and something of Florence in Ann; subconsciously perhaps he wrote himself and his marriage into these delightful tales. Coles was, as will be seen, something of a dilettante, and experimented in many fields. That he was happily married and fond of his family there can be no doubt, but when he lauded his wife's virtues to his friends and it later reached her ears she would say, 'I wish he would show it some time'. His daughter Mary was emphatic on this point. 'There was quite a lot of Ann in my mother and of Jan Stewer in my father. If he was in a very tricky situation of any description, she would say, "You can't do it that way", of which he would apparently take not the slightest notice—but one found that in actual fact he acted on the advice in the end.' Coles had (like Jan) a certain endearing other-worldliness. Florence scolded her husband a good deal less (though given no less cause) than Ann does Jan; her pet name for him was 'Sonny'. 'Jan's Paper-hanging' is one tale told by Mrs Stewer, and the action, predictably enough, is reminiscent of a Crazy Gang sketch or the old music-hall song 'When Father papered the Parlour'. The story has two significant features. First, there is a subtle change in the manner of the narrative in that, although the dialect is the same, the feminine note is sounded. It is slight but masterly. The second feature is Ann's deft and kindly handling of her man, which I suspect derives straight from Florence herself and the tactful way in which she sometimes handled her wilful and temperamental husband. 'The more I said to make 'n alter his mind the more determined he got,' said Ann. This may be said to be the story of Mrs Coles's life from the moment their marriage was mooted. 'Zome women don't know when 'tis time to stop terrifying a man, and they wonders that they gets traited bad. I'll admit a man is all the better for being taized a bit zometimes. But when it comes to too much aw't, then I reckon 'tis quite enough.' Ann ends: 'Arter a bit Jan come to his sainses; but he did'n do no more to papering. Us had in the tradesmen, and they scraped it all off and putt up fresh.'

Again like Jan, Coles was both conservative and a pioneer. I have always suspected that Jan, who has a proper respect for the 'bettermos' volk', would approve the verse excised from 'All things bright and beautiful' in today's hymn-books:

> The rich man in his castle,
> The poor man at his gate,
> God made them high and lowly
> And ordered their estate.

A. J. Coles, though he would not have gone thus far, was a Tory, open and unashamed. He was wise enough to keep political affinities out of his tales; only once did he slip up, when he allowed a character of left-wing tendencies to be described as 'not knowing Gurt A from a bule's voot'. This was during an election, and Coles's feelings temporarily got the better of him. It probably passed unnoticed by most of his readers, and he may even have been unaware of it himself.

Like Jan, Coles was fond of his pipe; like Jan, he was a moderate drinker and, like Jan, he sometimes spoke jokingly as if he were half-ashamed of it. Recalling his early days at Puddington, and the inspiration gained there and in its immediate surroundings for so many of his tales, A. J. C. referred to 'the people one met in the smithy, in the Black Dog, or the Angel, or the Ring o' Bells, or the—dear me, you will wonder where I picked up all those names.' And Jan says: ' 'Twas all the talk fer weeks ahead bout this-yer Cricket Match. Up to the Black 'Oss you cude'n yer nothing else—so they tells me.' The original title of this particular tale, by the way, was 'Jan's First and Last Cricket Match', and the story suggests that he had no intention of ever being engaged in such tom-foolery again. It would perhaps be more accurate to call it 'Jan's Immortal Cricket Match', for in one sense he has been destined to go on playing that match over and over again, through his imperishable Devon prose, as if it were some recurrent event in one of J. B. Priestley's time plays. I say 'destined' rather than 'doomed' because so forbidding a word cannot properly be used for a game which continues to give pleasure to generations of readers.

There was a certain childlike quality about A. J. C. reflected, I am sure quite unconsciously, in Jan Stewer, and which could sometimes degenerate into childish petulance. For example, he would rarely admit that he was in the wrong, even when it was demonstrably true. But the kinder and truer way of expressing this side of his nature is that A. J. C., like Jan, never grew out of a certain lovable youthfulness of heart. He would enter into games with his children as if he were no older than they were, and the family's Christmas parties were unique. He was not satisfied with the traditional games and would invent highly ingenious ones of his own, and if he arrived near the end of a children's party he would not hide his displeasure at having been left out. They soon learnt to time these events so that they were over before his return.

Florence was over thirty when she married A. J. C., and there was a strong love-hate relationship between them, with the ambivalence mostly on his side. The cliché about there being a strong woman behind every great man was certainly true in his case: he would have been nothing without her, and on many occasions she kept him from making a complete fool of himself. He was very affectionate and, though not demonstrative himself, was very angry indeed if it were not returned.

He was loved by some and heartily disliked by others. At home he could be the life and soul of the party, or like a bear with a sore head. If the latter was the case the whole family would do their best to keep out of his way, only to be accused of ganging up on him. Colin, I am told, was greatly embarrassed one evening when the members of a local amateur drama club were discussing who they would ask to produce their next play. Someone said, 'Why not ask Jan Stewer if he would produce for us?' and another member of the group, not knowing Colin was Coles's son, said, 'Good Lord, don't ask *him* for goodness sake, I can't stand the man.' A. J. C. laughed louder than anybody when this incident was repeated at home, but had he been in his 'other mood' he would have dared the family to go near that group again.

He never chastised his children, except with words; but these, used by a master, could be highly wounding. When she was twenty-three, Mary said to him, 'How can you be such a brute?' Highly indignant, Coles said 'How dare you! What do you think my father would have said if I had called him a brute?', to which she replied, 'Perhaps he wasn't one.' Yet he admired her for standing up to him. 'Brute' is a strong word to use of a man who was always desperately nervous before appearing on stage. Although he had been a soldier there was nothing of the stiff upper lip about him, and he wept copiously at the pathos in Charles Chaplin's *City Lights*. When there were violent rows in the household, ending with tears, A. J. C. would weep more copiously than any of them.

Throughout Coles's varied life, Florence was the organiser behind the scenes. He was grateful if she called his attention to a letter inviting him to perform at some function—but if it was a letter he had not wanted her to see, all hell was let loose. 'You should never have married an actor,' he would throw up at her. And she would truthfully reply, 'I didn't. I married a village schoolmaster.' Mary told me: 'If my mother smacked us and we cried and went to bed, she always came up and made peace.' He was vain and obstinate (like Jan); and in the early days of their marriage, when he was experimenting so successfully with amateur dramatics, the good-looking young man had some of the prettiest girls of Torquay at his feet. Meanwhile his wife was at home sitting at the sewing machine making dresses for these same girls to wear at the forthcoming production. He was the head of the household, and was quite definite on the point, but she remained the power behind the throne. It will be recalled that, filling in the census paper, Jan insists that he is head of the family. This brings from Ann the indignant question, 'If you be head, what be I then? Tail, I spause?'. 'Git along, mother,' says Jane. 'Of cou'se father's head o' the vam'ly on paaper.' And thus it was in the Coles household.

But there were lighter resemblances between Coles and Jan Stewer. When an office was built at the bottom of the garden of the family's Torquay house, a piece of asbestos was used to keep it against the back wall. As A. J. C., Mary and Joan were carrying the section to its new position, it slipped and fell on all their toes, laming them for some considerable time. They shouted with pain, and then with uncontrollable laughter. This particular incident did not appear in 'Jan Builds a House' in *Yap*, but it is hard to believe it did not in part inspire the story.

If the Jan of the books is life itself, the Jan of the stage was larger than life. (Here, though writing of Jan, the past tense must be used, for his stage self as portrayed by Coles could not survive his creator's death.) He appeared as the embodiment of every real and imagined comic rustic character, magnificently exaggerated. No smock, no straw between the teeth—that would have been too obvious a caricature for A. J. Coles—but dressed as authentically as any country farmer, with the most improbable addition of a frock-coat and top-hat. His every movement and quickly changing facial gestures were a delight. He was inimitably funny, slightly grotesque, and almost frightening in his impact, terrible as an army with banners.

The Jan Stewer of the books bears the same resemblance to the genuine old-fashioned farmer as Sam Weller does to the genuine Cockney of Dickens's day—that is to say he is as real as life and only slightly exaggerated. The Jan Stewer of the stage was both as probable and improbable a representation of the old-time rustic as was Shaw's representation of a real Cockney dustman in his hugely comic characterisation of Alfred Doolittle. Jan, with his stick, his make-up, his funny walk, his patter and his songs, was a figure straight out of Victorian music-hall, a sort of Devonshire Harry Lauder. True, the stage Jan had the same ear-to-ear beard and spare frame as the Jan of the books, but he also had a mop of unparted hair which Ann would never have allowed. He told the same stories and suffered the same indignities, but he was much more expansive. And whereas the Jan of the books telling you the story of the cricket match makes you chuckle, the stage Jan, telling it in the same words, made you roar with laughter. His face was never still: he imitated every character he mentioned to perfection—vocally, facially and bodily—which is quite beyond the more restrained page-Jan.

The stage Jan came fully into his own when he sang that uproariously comic song 'Out Come Mother and Me'. Here he had the field all to himself. He and 'Mother' stepped it out 'brave and fine', hand in hand, in all sorts of unexpected situations. Of course, you did not actually see 'Mother', but you almost did; you pictured her, too, as a slight caricature of the real thing, with her bonnet slightly awry. Jan and 'Mother' did things that the Jan and Ann you read about would never contemplate in their wildest dreams. They stepped out of the train on Muddlecombe Station and were mistaken for expected royalty (this, perhaps the song's funniest verse, was suggested by his son Harry); they went to a temperance meeting, and escaped the 'collection' by a magnificently cunning ruse of which the other Jan would be quite incapable. (If further proof were needed that the two Jans were distinct personalities, the first verse of this song provides it. Here Mrs Stewer's name was Susan, she had been in service in London, and her mistress provided the gown for the wedding in, of all places, Hanover Square.) The couple was quite unabashed by the fact that the waiting crowd was expecting a princess and at least a lord, and continued to step it out 'so brave and fine'. Being a Londoner Susan took him back to the city again to see the Lord Mayor's Show. They tagged themselves on to the procession and gaily acknowledged the cheers of the crowd with raised forefingers and gallant bows. No, this was not Ann, she would never countenance such behaviour; this was the grown-up, pert little Cockney maiden Susan.

Sequels are rarely as good as the originals and 'When Mother and Me Joined In' is no exception, lacking the other's element of anticlimax—

except, of course, when it was performed by its writer and composer, when it was every bit as funny. 'You'd never believe the diff'rence it made when Mother and me joined in' ended each chorus: they went to a modern dance, a choral society, a whist drive and a skating rink—this last episode, in the master's hands, was a riot, his teetering actions positively Chaplinesque.

'What About a Little Drop o' Cider?' was inspired by that question often being asked, during the Coles family's days at Five Mile Farm near Exeter, after a thorough survey of a neighbouring farm. It is in an entirely different genre from its two predecessors, and is straight out of Wurzel country.

It was when A. J. Coles was teaching at Poltimore that Jan Stewer first took on a physical appearance. Readers of the *Western Weekly News* had seen pictures of A. J. Coles, but they wanted to see what Jan Stewer looked like. In Poltimore lived William Sprague, with whom A. J. C. struck up a friendship. Sprague was cheery company, could sing a good song, was full of dry humour, and spoke in a rich Devon brogue. It was he who spruced himself up for the occasion, and it is his face, that of a somewhat solemn-looking, respectable old gentleman, that appears on the covers of the *Carrier's Van* series. Sprague died, when nearly ninety, at Stoke Canon, and he and his descendants were rightly proud of his being the inspirer of the Jan Stewer make-up.

But the stage Jan was an original—and it was his photograph that appeared in later issues of west-country papers. The beard was tousled, the hair was a mess, and he himself was the very Dan Leno of rusticity. He was, of course, a composite character of many rustics Coles had known, but Coles always acknowledged that if he had to name any one person as the prompter of the dialect sketches it would be the Puddington wheelwright whom he had been so proud to call his friend. Ned Knowles was a man with a quaint humour of which he himself was entirely unaware. He spoke rapidly in a beautiful dialect, and had the habit, when talking, of sliding his forefinger over the top of his right ear and under his nose in one quick motion—a mannerism which Coles early on incorporated into that mirth-provoking, awe-inspiring character, the Jan Stewer of the stage.

By this time, Coles relied entirely upon Jan Stewer for his livelihood. His temperament was such that he did not take easily to any task that tied him to a desk or ordered his comings and goings by a clock, and four years of army life had not made him more amenable to discipline. So he donned the wig and whiskers, the breeches and leggings, which figured in so many stage appearances, and began rehearsing stories, sketches and songs sufficient to constitute an evening's entertainment. His growing family was a captive audience for these rehearsals, and the children later assisted him by piano accompaniment, sketch versions of the monologues, or 'impromptu' gaps. But to begin with, Coles held the stage alone.

His first tentative stage appearance was on 25 January 1902, in a concert at the Victoria Hall, Queen Street, Exeter (later destroyed by fire). It was in aid of the Journalists' Widow's and Orphans Fund, and Jan's contribution was the cricket-match monologue. He had been advertised as 'the real Jan Stewer', and Mr Gratwicke, that year's president of the Institute of Journalists, arranged the concert. At one point, Gratwicke crept along the orchestra and in a stage whisper urged Jan to speak up, an occurrence which Coles remembered ever afterwards with mixed feelings. His daughter described this debut as 'a fiasco', but it must go down in this biography as a climactic point in the Jan Stewer saga.

During the next few years he toured most of the towns and large villages of Devon and Cornwall and a part of Somerset—sometimes appearing at three, four or five different places. The compere of each show was A. J. Coles, in boiled shirt and tails, introducing it with a description of Muddlecombe and its notable features, institutions (especially the Black 'Oss), the oldest inhabitant, and so on. He would make two or three appearances: giving solos on a one-string fiddle made from a cigar box, a ventriloquist's sketch with Old Peter (his dummy), and a memory act. This last act would put most modern performers to shame for, relying on a highly ingenious use of mnemonics, he would not only remember each of thirty objects but also the order in which they had been listed. For example, if the fifteenth object was a champagne bottle, he would associate it with the fifteen members of a rugby team celebrating their success with a bottle of champagne. The star of the show, of course, was Jan—and he played to every type of audience from royalty to gaol inmates. After the death of A. J. Coles, Old Peter had to be destroyed, having contracted woodworm, but the beard (somewhat shrunken through constant combing) and wig were preserved.

A. J. Coles was as unbusiness-like as Jan, and in those early days he fell an easy victim to requests to perform on behalf of charities he had never even heard of. His vanity was flattered and he was soon contributing, as he expressed it himself in later years, 'to almost every conceivable good cause from painting the parish pump to procuring new uniforms for the town band'. Although a refund of travelling expenses was customarily offered, such appearances involved travelling no small distance and forgoing his fees. If the occasion was a charity bazaar or jumble sale, not only was he expected to make a purchase but he also forfeited prospective business, since by performing in a place for the benefit of other people he surrendered the opportunity of performing there for his own sake. Slowly it dawned on him that a line would have to be drawn somewhere. So he later agreed to perform without a fee only where no charge was made for admission, which still left hospitals, public institutions, old age pensioners' parties, homes for the aged or afflicted, and the like.

Usually letters of request were couched in pleading terms difficult to resist. But not always. One such petition came from members of a Nonconformist body in a small west-country town: in a long letter they gave a detailed description of the church they were planning to build and the estimated cost, with a complete statement of the funds in hand and in view. The scheme proposed for correcting the disparity between the two was an evening's entertainment by Jan Stewer, which they were good enough to say would be 'a great draw'. They said their committee was willing to defray his travelling expenses and provide hospitality for the night, but it was left in no doubt that they expected to have his performance free of charge. They even went so far as to mention some of the distinguished people likely to be present. This was enough to upset what Peter Gurney used to call his 'Equal Abraham'. (Gurney was one of Coles's many fictional villagers, derived from the third name of the 'Widecombe Fair' chorus; or, as Jan explains, 'Turney Gurney as us always calls 'en, on account of his being abble to spaichify 'pon any subjic' whether he knows aught about it or no, and use sitch long words.' He rarely takes any action in the stories—an exception being 'Every Man to His Trade'—but is usually introduced in the context of a quotable quote beginning, 'As Turney Gurney use to zay . . .'). Coles had never visited the abovementioned town before, knew no one there and had no personal interest in its institutions. It would, in the course of time, have been included in his professional circuit, but had he given his show there for nothing he would have had to cut it out of his future itinerary. An urgent footnote to the letter volunteered the information that if the committee could raise an additional £500 they would be able to buy and equip a graveyard for the proposed building. At this, Coles saw red and replied to the effect that, while he regretted being unable to accept the engagement, if the committee would let him know when the graveyard was ready he would suggest a couple of people that might be buried in it. Negotiations went no further.

In response to a moving appeal he did go to another town, this time entirely at his own expense, and gave a performance lasting nearly an hour. 'Jan Stewer' had been widely billed in large type, and the hall was full. A few days later he received a letter from the promoters saying that as the concert had been such a success they proposed to repeat it, and asking him to come and give a second performance. He suggested, in response, that on this occasion he be paid a fee. There was no reply. Yet sometimes he would return home with a cheque for payment in his pocket, which lay untouched until, much later, his more practical wife discovered it—further evidence of A. J. C. and Florence being written, though probably unconsciously, into Jan and Ann Stewer.

Paid or unpaid, Jan Stewer fast became a feature of west-country towns and villages. Last-minute preparations often had to be made, the songs being accompanied by pianists of varied accomplishment. (Here, as already noted, members of the family came in useful when they were older.) The 'dressing-room' was once so stuffy that Coles promptly took off his shoe and smashed a hole in the window; his explanation of 'a slight accident' was happily accepted.

Harry began accompanying his father when he was half-way through his teens. Once they went to a small Cornish town and, upon arrival at the hall, made their customary inspection: A. J. C. the stage, lighting and dressing-room, Harry the piano. 'This piano', groaned Harry, 'is a one-way instrument. The keys go down but flatly refuse to come up again.' On removing the back, the inside of the piano was found to be, like the walls of the room, dripping wet. Just then a small boy put his head in at the door, and Harry offered him free admission if he would bring them as many newspapers as he could carry. He soon returned, with so many papers that he had to walk crab-fashion in order to see where he was going. He and A. J. C. spent the next ten minutes twisting the pages into ropes, which Harry lit and then waved to and fro over the mechanism of the piano until it was thoroughly hot and dried out. This allowed over half the keys to work, which Harry described as a 'majority verdict'.

Another piano (in a North Devon village) produced, during Harry's customary trial run, a good impression of a duet between a broken-down barrel organ and a pair of cymbals. Several wires had gone adrift and, resting across others, twanged every chord to a jangling edge. Some notes retained all their original wires while others had only one, giving the tunes a queer imbalance. A piano-tuner was found, who spent an hour removing one wire from any place where there were three and fitting it in where there was only one, thus converting the instrument to a bi-chord action. This worked fairly well, except that one or two of the newly stretched wires expressed their resentment by snapping disconcertingly during the performance.

These 'one-night stands' were even more hazardous when a local accompanist had to be relied on. Inevitably, many arrangements had to be made in advance, and at one village the hall caretaker, who was also the village carpenter, undertook to make them all. But when A. J. C. arrived he saw, on his way to the hall, not one of the bills he had sent ahead to be posted on hoardings, walls or shop windows. When he was located and asked what had happened to the printing, the caretaker said, 'Aw, I was waiting to see what you wanted done with it', and blithely produced bills, circulars and window-cards, all as good as new. When A. J. C. gasped, 'But the performance is this evening', he said blandly 'Aw, is it?'. That he had completely overlooked the show was clear upon arrival at the hall. Chairs were heaped in wry embrace in odd corners and all over the stage, and the unswept floor was littered with scraps of paper, cigarette ends, empty cartons, nut shells and bits of orange peel. There was no sign of the promised footlights or curtains, the piano was at the wrong end of the room, and the oil-lamps were untrimmed.

'Aw,' said the caretaker, 'if you want the place put straight, you say so.' Coles said so, and the hall was more or less ready in time for the performance. With a borrowed bottle of ink and a pointed stick, A. J. C. hastily scrawled 'Tonight' in large letters on each bill and offered a bright-looking boy a shilling to get them displayed in as many places as he could. This lad earned his money: one was even hung on the handle of the village pump. Asked 'How about our accompanist for the piano?' the carpenter-caretaker replied, 'Aw, you can't do better than Ben Daggle. Nobody can't touch he for musicking. He do's all the piano playing round these parts.' 'You've booked Mr Daggle have you?' 'Aw, no. I didn't like to interfere. I thought you'd be the best one to do that.'

A. J. C. hurried to Mr Daggle's cottage, opposite the church, only to be told by his mother that he was away playing at a dance in a village seven miles away. She suggested the lady 'who plays the organ to the chapel', who lived opposite the post office. She was in—and appeared to be about sixty-five, but a venerable, Victorian sixty-five. She was silver-haired with vertical curls flanking her forehead, of spare frame, primly set features and thin straight lips. She wore a black dress fastened up to the neck, a tiny black silk apron, lace-fringed, and a sweet white mob-cap with a bow of coffee-coloured ribbon. She seemed to go with antimacassars, a walnut what-not, a neatly contrived patchwork quilt, a multi-coloured sampler and, certainly, the chapel organ. She was not quite what Coles was looking for, but he was desperate. He could see her features were taking shape for a polite dismissal, until he mentioned the magic name 'Jan Stewer'; she turned out to be an avid reader of his tales. She agreed to try over the songs, he placed 'Out Come Mother and Me' on her music rack, she gazed at it long and earnestly, and then said, 'Oh dear'. She suggested trying someone else, but time was running out and the hall had still to be prepared, so she was persuaded. When she played the introduction it was the first time, Coles said later, that he had noticed how much his setting resembled a

Moody and Sankey hymn. At the end of the half-hour they were still rehearsing the first verse. But the show had to go on, and they went, fearfully, to the hall. He went on stage wearied and worried, and with two hours to fill; she sat in the centre of the front row, impressively gowned in a beautiful black silk dress dating, he guessed, from about 1870, with a neat crinoline skirt and a small bonnet which dangled a number of jet ornaments like tiny swaying bells. He postponed the songs as long as he dared—he talked about Muddlecombe, its gossip and tittle-tattle, he told all the stories he could think of and did some longer sketches. But 'Out Come Mother and Me' was featured on the programme, so finally he announced it and expressed his indebtedness to the lady who, at such short notice, had consented to play for him. To loud applause she ascended the stage and arranged herself on the piano stool, during which operation, which was quite a lengthy one, he donned the Jan Stewer wig and whiskers.

She played the introduction *adagio* and with great deliberation. He began singing but, do what he would, he could not slow down the words to keep pace with her. He tried to do so for a couple of lines, then gave up and went ahead on his own. When he started on the 'repeat' of the rather lengthy chorus, he realised the accompanist was now part-way through the first chorus. Could they finish together? Cocking his ear to the piano he tried to gauge his speed so that this might be done, estimating that he must sing a trifle less than two bars to one. He became quite excited. At the same time he sensed something was going on in the row of 'stalls' where two or three ladies were seated who, he later discovered, were very musical and also very sporting. They caught his purpose and excitement, and entered into the spirit of it: glancing backwards and forwards from singer to player they exchanged little animated gasps and exclamations as they eagerly watched the progress of the race. Then they discovered that he knew that they knew, and they were all in it. It was great fun, and he brought it off—in a triumph of timing he finished precisely on the last note of the accompaniment, but one lap ahead. The ladies applauded vociferously. He hastened to the piano and turned back the music to the beginning, indicating to the accompanist that she now begin again, and for all three verses they did it: started together, parted company and then finished, a dead heat, at the winning post.

Coles was usually more fortunate in his accompanists than on that occasion. Seventy-seven-year-old Mrs Winifred Alford recalled how she played for him during a week's tour, in the 1920s, at Exbourne, Inwardleigh, Hatherleigh and Okehampton. In her early twenties at the time, she was a well-known pianist locally. She clearly remembered the 'real gentleman', in dress suit, of the first half of the act and the same man, scarcely recognisable in Jan Stewer's full regalia, in the second half—the indiarubber face, the songs, the patter, and the artistry she largely found lacking in most modern entertainers. 'Nothing we have today could touch him.' Young Winifred Thompson, as she then was, was a clerk in the rural district offices at Okehampton, and her employer made it quite clear that he· considered it slightly 'infra dig.' for her to be taking part in such a frivolous affair as a Jan Stewer concert. But he came to the tour's last performance at the Praetoria Hotel, Okehampton, to see her presented by the star of that one-man show with a box of chocolates. Coles was still dressed as Jan, and the box was in a 'bundle' which he carefully unwrapped. 'I expect it was his "rid pocket-ankcher",' said Mary when I told her.

It was thus that Coles learnt and mastered his craft. It may sound amateurish, but it was in fact masterly. During the First World War, the stage Jan became almost instantly popular; Coles found himself performing at halls in Portsmouth, Southampton and Eastleigh, and at Netley Hospital. While still a corporal in training at Aldershot, he was soon installed as 'O.C. Entertainments': one room was used as a theatre, and a piano was hired for the three months he was there.

Twice on the stage Jan performed before royalty. The first time was on 20 May 1921, when he made the speech of welcome to the then Prince of Wales (later to become Edward VIII and, after abdication, the Duke of Windsor) on his visit to an 'Old English Fair' in aid of the hospital at the Drill Hall, Plymouth. He came on in full regalia of corduroys and whiskers, and delivered his greeting on behalf of the Devon and Cornish assembly in broad dialect. He never forgot the quizzical expression on the Prince's face as he regarded him keenly with humorous eyes, doubtless trying to comprehend what it was all about.

The second occasion was on 17 May 1938, when Queen Mary was the guest of Lord Mildmay of Flete for five days. The performance was to take place in the music room, and A. J. Coles and his daughter Joan arrived in good time. The grand piano was on the floor, below and to the right of the stage. Joan went down the stairs in a becoming gown secured for the occasion, and her father remained above on the balcony, as he intended making his first appearance, in white coat and tails, through the curtains when the members of the audience were all seated. He had anticipated a large audience, but when he peeped through the curtains he realised that this was to be an intimate house-party audience of no more than some fourteen people. All at once he felt frightened and inept: the party he had to entertain for half an hour consisted almost entirely of titled ladies and gentlemen, one of them a queen. Few, if any, he thought, had ever encountered the rustic tongue—the dialect jokes would surely misfire. When the familiar opening bars of 'Widecombe Fair' struck up, he went down the stairs feeling like a condemned man going to the gallows.

But he had reckoned without Queen Mary. She began clapping as soon as he stepped on the stage, and all joined in; which gave him a chance to get his breath. He still refused to be comforted, and for the first few minutes he said his lines mechanically. As it happened, he was a roaring success. But he had a further fear: the next part of the act was the sketch version of the census-paper monologue, and although his daughter went to her dressing-room to make up as the old woman he felt he dare not leave the stage. He opted for changing only above the belt; Jan's coat, red neckerchief, wig and whiskers would suffice to create the illusion. So, while explaining with impromptu patter the stage set the audience would have to imagine, he brought on his clothes from the wings, removed his coat and waistcoat and, still talking, donned those of Jan. The audience was highly amused. The wig and whiskers he left to the last when, apologising for turning his back, he slipped them on in two quick movements and turned to the front again. There was laughter and applause. (From that time on he made the visible change part of the act.) After the ordeal was over the Queen assured him she had been amused by the account of Jan's first and last cricket match, and complimented Joan on her performance in 'Jan and the Census Paper'.

I once saw Jan perform, between the First and Second World Wars, at Hartland Abbey Fete. It was in the open air, seats were arranged for the audience and, this being a money-raising event, extra tickets had to be bought for the performance. Making his way towards the piece of ground that served as a stage, Coles was stopped by the man in charge of collecting tickets, who greeted him with the peremptory assertion, 'You can't come in without yer ticket.' Coles began muttering something about his being the performer, but the man persisted, ' 'Tis no gude, I tell 'ee. You can't come yer unless I takes yer ticket.' For a moment I thought Coles was going to explode with indignation, but instead—faced with the real thing, so to speak—he exploded with laughter.

The stage appearances continued—not only all over the west country, but also in Bristol, Bath, Swansea and the Midlands—in church halls, village schoolrooms and (gratis!) at police concerts. But not until twenty years after his first tentative performance at Exeter could he pluck up courage to perform in that city again. A personal friend, Mr Alik Guest, arranged a couple of recitals for him at the Barnfield Hall (now Theatre), and the house was filled on each occasion. It must have been many years after that, following the Second World War, that I saw Jan in the Buller Hall, both in person and in a film which belongs to another chapter.

The identification of A. J. Coles with Jan Stewer was now complete. One day A. J. Coles had occasion to go into Exeter's general post office; it was pouring with rain, and he went there by car. It was in a no-parking area, but he took the chance and inside found himself at the end of a long queue. When he came outside again, he found himself facing a stern-looking policeman. 'Are you aware no parking is allowed here, sir?' 'Yes, constable, I know; but I expected my call to be a much shorter one than proved to be the case.' 'I see. May I see your driving licence, sir?'

It was produced and handed over. The constable opened it, and read out the name A. J. Coles. He handed it back. 'I'm not getting my notebook wet for you, Jan Stewer. Off you go.'

FIVE

Teacher

Like Joseph the dreamer, A. J. Coles had a coat of many colours—or, to change the Old Testament metaphor to a New Testament one, many talents. To only a few men is it given to possess even one outstanding gift—and most of them bury it in the ground. A. J. Coles was a man of great versatility, and being something of a dilettante he moved from one field to another with remarkable dexterity. Coles's early teaching career was of no small relevance to the development of his later vocation, and it is worthwhile looking at the inter-relation of the two in a little detail.

His career as a schoolmaster, as already described, began in the little village of Puddington in the late 1890s. Today the school, and the schoolhouse almost opposite it, must look much as they did when Coles tentatively began to teach there. There was no question of his being the headmaster with a staff of teachers under him, or of being one of such a staff himself. It was a one-man job.

Six months after he had taken charge of the school, the average attendance had risen to an extent which made the prospect of an addition to the next government grant—the criterion of success or failure—seem reasonable. At a meeting of the school managers, the rector proposed that the good work put in by the master be repaid by an increase to £100 a year. The motion was received sympathetically by all but one farmer, who rose in wrath. 'What?' he exclaimed. 'I shan't agree to no such thing. Why, darn 'ee, I can get a chap to do a man's work for fifteen shillings a week, and you'm telling about paying two pound a week for a feller to sit all day on his backside. I won't bide yer and hearken to it.' And he stomped out. Four years later, when A. J. C. was appointed headmaster of a much larger school at Teignmouth, this same man was one of a group of parents and grandparents who proposed to make his salary up to that of the new post if he stayed on at Puddington. The newly married teacher declined the offer and went to Teignmouth.

Here he accepted the temporary post (for one year) of headmaster of Exeter Road Boys' School: having started with forty scholars, he now had charge of over 300. It was a happy year, and Coles and his wife made many friends. But they found themselves living uneasily in one of a row of houses which all looked exactly alike, so much so that a potentially embarrassing incident occurred on their first evening there. They had been hard at work all day brushing, cleaning, unpacking cases, spreading carpets, sweeping up shavings and hauling furniture. A. J. C. had not been slow in finding the location of the nearest pub and, assuring himself that nobody was in sight, he scurried across the street in his shirt-sleeves and bought two bottles of beer. He then dashed back with one under each arm, darted into the house and across the miniature hall, burst open the door—and found himself in a room full of strangers. The shock of surprise reduced everyone to a gaping silence, in the midst of which he vanished as quickly as he had appeared and returned to his own house next door. He never got further than a nodding acquaintance with those neighbours, and they probably never knew who it was that appeared in their house and disappeared again with such suddenness.

The Exeter Road school building was demolished in 1975, but the school continues in another part of the town. Over the years successive headmasters kept log-books, and the one kept by Coles during his short tenure was fuller than that of any other head for a similar period. Fortunately these have been preserved, and the following quotations may be of interest. (All are from the year 1902.)

January 6. School reopened after Xmas Vacation. I commenced duty as head master. A. J. Coles.

January 20. The uncle of the boy B. called this morning to say he was unable to make the lad attend school. I advised him to use a little physical persuasion as otherwise he would be summoned.

January 24. This afternoon an official of the Great Western Ry. called and spoke to the boys on the danger of throwing stones at passing trains.

January 29. The boy E. J. being away and unable to get a satisfactory reason from his brother I sent him home for a better one. His father called and it eventually transpired that the boy is not very well. I pointed out to the father the folly of parents trying to act in a manner antagonistic to the teacher.

February 18. The mother of the boy D. called, complaining of the treatment the boy had received from his teacher. On investigation I found that the injuries received were not inflicted by the teacher, but that the boy had been abusive, and kicked R. Hobbs, the pupil teacher.

March 1. A new school year commences. I have transferred 6 boys to the lower school to bring our numbers back to 180. I have introduced an 'attendance ladder' of my own make to encourage the children to attend well.

March 2. The attendance ladder seems to be a success, and the children are keen on climbing. The percentage today is 97.

March 7. School closed today in order to give the children an opportunity of viewing the royal train.

April 11. A report that peace had been proclaimed in South Africa was spread through the town this morning, and special editions of the morning papers being issued containing the news, which was generally accepted as true, a half holiday was given in the afternoon.

April 18. Administered exceptional punishment to S.T. Std VI, this morning for insubordination. Punishment consisted of 3 strokes of cane on either hand. (In spite of entries such as this, Harry Coles says that his father was by no means a lifelong advocate of corporal punishment—another example of his being ahead of his times as a teacher.)

April 28. The use of paper or books instead of slates in Standard I is strongly recommended.

June 2. News of Peace having arrived yesterday (Sunday) the children of the three departments in this school formed a procession in the morning and marched to the Den, where patriotic songs and the National Anthem were sung. A gentleman at the East Devon Club sent out sufficient sweets to be given all round. A holiday was given in the afternoon.

June 3. Pictorial Cards in celebration of the termination of the Boer War were given to the children of all schools in Teignmouth today by Mr and Mrs S. A. Croydon.

August 25. I have commenced to teach a few of the boys and some of the girls from the girls' department the children's operetta entitled 'Mr Nobody' to be performed at the Teignmouth School of Art Fete on Thursday next at Bitton.

August 27. I took the children taking part in 'Mr Nobody' to Bitton this morning for a rehearsal.

August 29. At the Teignmouth Sch. of Art Fete yesterday the operetta 'Mr Nobody' was performed by 9 boys and 7 girls from this school. The children acquitted themselves very creditably. The whole thing was prepared and the parts learned in a week.

On 20 September he reported that he had sent a notice 'Illegal Employment of Children Notice to Employers' to a local man who was employing a boy 'for the purpose of picking winkles'.

At the end of the year, A. J. C. and his wife returned gratefully to village life when he took charge of the school at Poltimore, five miles from Exeter. There he bought a motor-bicycle, the first one seen in the village. In those days these machines were as smelly as they are still noisy, and when he roared his way through the lanes and the village street mothers would rush out to drag their children to safety. A sort of bath-chair trailer which could be hitched on behind it allowed his wife and infant to be hauled around the countryside, though he had to dismount to push the whole unwieldy outfit up anything more than a moderate rise. At Poltimore, he found himself living next door to the home of the parents of Charles Wreford, another reciter of stories in the Devon dialect. He and Wreford were also to share in radio broadcasts of their narratives.

His next and last appointment was as a teacher at Bovey Tracey, where he was in charge of the British School for two years. He lived in Newton Abbot during this period and cycled to and fro the six miles each day, having sold what was left of the motor-bicycle after what he described as 'one or two misunderstandings with objects bigger than myself'.

His teaching methods were unorthodox and sometimes brought him into sharp conflict with the educational authorities of the time. He was an obstinate man, and stuck to his guns. Not only was he ahead of his times, but even today there would be those who would look askance at his deliberate use of the Devonshire dialect as a tool in his English literature classes. For A. J. Coles, as perhaps hardly needs to be said, loved the Devonshire dialect. One day, when travelling by train to London, he overheard a lady in the same carriage remark to her husband, 'It's beautiful country, no denying that, but isn't it dreadful that with all this free education, the people in those villages should speak such terrible English?' This touched him on a particularly sore point; and as they neared Salisbury, he imagined the same lady standing before Stonehenge and protesting, 'Isn't it a scandal that after all these years of public authorities and government departments the place should be littered up with these untidy stones!' Only his innate courtesy made him hold his peace.

But when another teacher at a remote Devon village school inquired in despairing tones, 'What can be done to cure the children of this dreadful dialect?' he replied, 'Not very much, thank goodness. It is not dreadful and it shouldn't be cured.' 'Only endured?' 'No. Taught.' And he went on to make it quite clear that he would make it a punishable offence for any teacher to give the children cause to suppose that the native speech of their forefathers was something to be regretted, still less to be eradicated. On the contrary, they should be led to perceive how much in it was dignified, beautiful, historic and romantic. To this end, all teachers should be examined in their proficiency in the dialect of their own district.

Thus, all those years ago, he was teaching quite a few rustic youngsters to speak at least moderately good English by using their native dialect as a foundation. He would say to the class, 'Greet me in good Devon, and inquire after my health.' And they would respond, 'Gude morning, how be yu?' or 'How be gettin' vore?' or 'How be knackin' along?' Then he would ask for the same question in 'correct' English, and they would say, 'Good morning, how are you?' Or he might reverse the order, and ask a scholar to translate into Devon, 'Where are you going with that great stump of a tree?' To which the lad would reply, 'Where be gwain wi' thikky gurt moot?' This would produce a roar of laughter from the class—and any teacher unable to do so has undoubtedly mistaken his vocation. He would then cunningly work in some English literature and quote from Chaucer:

From thilke assembly if I may
Shall no man warn me today.

In many places were nightingales
Alpes, finches and wodewales,
That in her sweet song delighten
In thilke place as they habyten.

Saint Austin will thereto accord
In thilke book that I record.

He would point out that the 'l' might well have been silent, as in 'walk' or 'talk'; and that to make the lines scan correctly it was sometimes necessary to say 'thik' and sometimes 'thikee' as in pure Devon dialect.

He would write on the board, 'They tetties is comin' up suant,' and ask his pupils to correct the pronoun and verb and spell the vegetable properly. They would then write, 'Those potatoes are coming up—evenly, regularly, uniformly, level.' By such means they would painlessly pick up such words as 'obsolete', 'traditional', 'colloquial', 'archaic', 'classic', 'historic', 'romantic'.

Consider, too, how he taught them the meaning of the word 'metathesis'. He would write on the blackboard, 'Tommy, urn across the burge and apse the chicken-house door'. Asked to render this in 'good' English, the pupils would substitute 'run', 'bridge' and 'asp'; and with little prompting would observe that in each case the vowel and consonant sounds had changed places. When A. J. C. invited them to supply other dialect forms, these would come fast enough: burches, curst, girn, wapse, Kursmas, gurdge, crips (meaning breeches, crust, grin, wasp, Christmas, grudge and crisp). He would then quote Chaucer again:

The briddes how they singen clere
The mavis and the nightingale
And other joly briddes smale.

Told that such a transition was metathesis, the pupils added the word quite naturally to their vocabulary.

He would write on the blackboard: 'I worked as long as 'twas daylight, and tho I went home.' This is pure Devon. But it is also pure Chaucer:

Forth without words mo
In at the wicket went I tho.

Students of Chaucer will realise that he uses 'tho' for 'then' ; 'Tho 'gan I walk through the mead'; 'Now, good sir, quoth I right tho'. Dialect, insisted Coles, was the custodian, not the despoiler.

He would write on the board : 'You shouldn't have took that all to-once; you should have went to-twice.' He would then ask them to translate. This was English not only without tears, but with laughter.

He would, for a lesson on personal pronouns, recite the story of the little brother and sister who, on returning from the market town told their mother how they thought they had seen Auntie Bessie in the street. He would write on the board their description of the encounter: 'Us looked to she and her looked to we.' This was how they had been expressing themselves throughout their short lives, and they had taken it for granted. But to see it in the teacher's handwriting, disentangle it and get it straight in the parallel column was a cause of mirth. He would invite them to suggest other misuses of pronouns and write the correct form underneath; or he would say a phrase in dialect, and ask the children to repeat in correct English as quickly as possible. Thus:

Where be to? (Where are you?)
Let 'n bide where he's to. (Leave it where it is.)
Be gwain or no? (Are you going or not?)
You'm proper mazed. (You are completely out of your mind, foolish, silly, daft.)

Examples became progressively more advanced as the pupils increased in efficiency. The real fun came in the second half of the game, when the teacher gave the examples in the accepted tongue and the class provided the dialect equivalent.

We caught a mole. (Us ketched a want.)
Close the door and latch it. (Put vast thikky door and 'apse 'n.)
Tom and I will teach you. (Me and Tom'll larn 'ee.)

All exercises in this lesson were done in both languages. Thus 'I am, we are, thou art, you are, he is, they are,' became 'I be, us be, thee art, you'm (or you be), 'er is, they'm (or they be)'. The children gradually became bilingual. Walking across the playground, he would hear one of them come out with a broad colloquialism and the others burst out laughing, repeating the expression as a great joke. Such sorrows as he might have were lightened as he saw his methods bearing fruit.

He found out that he could get on well with children but, like many before and after him, he lacked the patience to deal with school managers and obdurate parents to whom his unorthodox methods were anathema. Yet at least one civil servant testified that, but for his tuition in Bovey Tracey and A. J. C.'s intervention with his parents on his behalf, he would probably have ended his days as a farm-hand.

While at Bovey Tracey, Coles would sometimes slip over to a cottage where the good lady would give him a glass of milk. This happened once when a school inspector paid an unexpected visit, and the following conversation ensued:

'It is directly against the rules for the master to leave the premises during school hours. I shall put this in my report.' 'How did you find out where I was?' 'The boys told me.' 'How were they behaving?' 'Surprisingly, they were all hard at work.' 'Will you put that in your report too?' They later became firm friends.

When a London journalist referred to him as 'that famous authority on the Devon dialect' Coles modestly disclaimed the description. He said he merely wrote what he heard and what his grandmother said, adding that his acquaintance with the etymological side of the matter was possibly more meagre than that of many of his readers. He said, 'I am not able to state, as some people are, whose works I read with the greatest respect, whether a dialect form is derived from a Saxon root which looks a cross between a sneeze and a stammer, or from a still older Celtic word which one can only pronounce properly with the hiccups.'

The truth is that this was another strand in his coat of many colours, and the fact that he was able to teach without tears in no way detracts from his expertise and knowledge. Let him put it in his own way:

'Fitty' has a significance quite distinct from 'suant'. The latter applies to form and order, while the former attaches to propriety. A dance at a wedding would be fitty, but if inexpertly performed might not go suant; a dance at a funeral, however well carried out, might go suant but would certainly not be fitty.

Whence came 'fitty'? A little while ago I had a fit of reading Geoffrey Chaucer, the father of English poetry, who certainly wrote the most refined English of his day. And his day was more than 500 years ago. Moreover, he was not a Devonian, but a Midlander.

I was struck with the number of words common to 'Dan' Chaucer and Jan Stewer; words which were then obviously current in the very best society, but which now are frowned upon or laughed at as 'dialect'. With regard to 'fitty', Chaucer frequently employs the word 'fetys' in exactly the same sense.

So noble he was of his stature,
So fair, so jolly, and so fetys.

A little key fetys enough
Which was of gold polished clear.

Upon this door I 'gan to smite
That was so fetys and so light.

Coles took the liberty of putting the other words in modern spelling; and then, with great pertinence, he asked if he should also write 'fitty' for 'fetys'. If so, he suggested, it surely gave their dialect form a dignity and placed them under a debt to all the 'Jan Stewers' who had preserved it.

He also defended the dialect form 'hobbidy-hoy' as against 'hobbledehoy', which many supposed to be the more correct form. At concerts and political meetings, more frequent in the pre-television days of his prime, the village youths would sometimes punctuate the proceedings with their own irreverent comments, at which someone might say, 'Don't take no notice of they, maister. 'Tis only a parcel of hobbidy-hoys.' This, he insisted, was no mere slipshod habit of speech leading to the alteration of words from their true form. There are, he pointed out, several ancient uses of the words which supported the 'Black 'Oss' usage rather than that of the BBC: 'hobbard-de-hoy', 'hobet-a-hay' and 'habber-de-hoy' occurred, but, so far as he knew, no 'hobble'. As an old friend of his said, in reference to another matter, 'Some book-larnid body put that in.' He quoted Tusser's *Hundred Good Points*, published in about 1570, which includes the following:

The first seven years bring up as a child,
The next to learning, for waxing too wild,
The next, keep under Sir Hobbard-de-hoy;
The next a man, no longer a boy.

'We shall', commented Coles, 'have to be a little more careful how we accuse these old people of "murdering good English." '

He quoted several good dialect words which were considered, centuries ago, to be pure English. One such was 'ballad': today, he pointed out, this was confined to the drawing-up of a programme for concerts, all vocal exercises being otherwise lumped together as 'songs'. Yet, he continued, grandfather out at Muddlecombe would still say, 'Sing us up a bit of a ballad.' Similarly, he defended the farm wife's use of 'brandies' when referring to the three-legged iron stand on which the pot rested over the log fire. Better-educated people might condescendingly say that what she really meant was 'brandiron'; but, Coles pointed out, the Anglo-Saxon form was 'brandisen'. This reminded him of 'fire-new':

'Got a fresh incubator, Jan, I see. Where did you get that one? To a sale?'
'No, begad. He's fire-new.'

To those who smiled indulgently at this expression, Coles gently pointed out that Shakespeare did not think that the correct expression was 'brand new': 'You should have accosted her,' says Fabian to Sir Andrew in *Twelfth Night*, 'with some excellent jests, fire-new from the mint.' Coles also pointed out that the poet also spoke of 'fire-new fortune', and that Queen Margaret shrivelled up Dorset with 'Peace, master marquis, you are malapert. Your fire-new stamp of honour is scarce current.'

Another country expression is (or at any rate was) a 'crowner's inquest'. If city folk smiled at this, Coles reminded them that Shakespeare's gravedigger, preparing the last resting-place of Ophelia, assured his companion, 'The Crowner hath sat on her and found it Christian burial'; and when asked, 'But is't law?' replied, 'Ay, marry is't, Crowner's quest law.' Years ago, Coles continued, he heard old people speak of the 'crouder': 'There's gwain to be dancing; the crouder have started.' This, he explained, was an ancient type of fiddle. Sir Philip Sidney, who (Coles said) was thinking of leaving off when Shakespeare started, said in his *Apologie for Poetrie*: 'I never heard the olde song of Percy and Duglas that I found not my heart moved more than with a trumpet; yet is it sung but by some blind crouder.' Yet another example is 'dandyprat', a word used to describe a 'swell'. This too, Coles said, was not just dialect; it appeared in quite serious literature of Elizabethan times.

He referred to the old cottage woman saying affectionately to her romping grandchild: 'You young Jezebel, you!' This might seem to have been merely an unfortunate choice of playful nickname, but Coles was not so sure. He did not think the grandmother had in mind the rather questionable lady who shared King Ahab's throne. What he believed she was really calling the child, though probably she did not know it, was 'dowsabell', a common term in the Middle Ages for 'sweetheart', which derived from the French *douce et belle* (sweet and beautiful). In support of this, he quoted not only Michael Drayton, a friend of Shakespeare who wrote the ballad of a dowsabell, but also a writer in a London journal of over 300 years ago: 'It were not good to cast away as pretty a dowsabell as one could see in a summer day.'

He also observed—and it is still the case—that the Devonian always 'makes a light' and 'makes' it out. The educated person 'puts' out the light. 'How does he do it?' Coles asked. 'I would invite anybody to examine the two expressions in cold blood. "Make out the light." Make it to be out. There's sense in that as well as dignity. But "Put out the light"! I ask you.' He further illustrated this point by observing that you can put out your tongue, put out the car and put out the jug for milk, but he defied anybody to put out the light. A 'correct-speaking' person was quite capable of saying,

'John, put out a light so that the visitors can see the way through the garden, but take care that you don't put it out.' With a sort of growing exasperation, he went on:

And just see to what extremes we will go rather than use the old Devonian's common sense expression 'Make a light.' Sometimes 'Strike a light;' sometimes 'Switch on a light;' but most times 'Light a light!' You can say 'Light a light' in a crowd of educated people without raising a smile; but if Jan says, 'Make a light' they'll take it home to amuse the neighbours. Ye gods!

Note has already been taken of his use of metathesis in his teaching. He brings this out amusingly in one of his Jan Stewer tales, when he says of Reginald Tooke at the fancy-dress ball that he was supposed to be 'Ossifer of State, or some sitch thing'. I am not aware that he has any Shakespearian or Chaucerian authority for this one! However, he brought in Chaucer to defend Jan's use of 'afore' in such expressions as, 'Never sit down afore you'm axed.' Chaucer had sung:

For such another as I guess
Afore ne'er was.

But what about 'axed'? Coles again quotes the cultured Chaucer:

I thanked her as best I might
And axed her how that she was hight
And what she was I axede, eke.

Chaucer had written:

... not a penny had in world
Although that she her clothes had sold,
And though she should anhonged be.

'Anhonged' meant 'hungry'—and, said Coles, Jan was always hungered, never hungry: 'I be that hungered I could eat a man off his hoss.' To quote 'The Fancy Dress Ball' again: rude comments were made upon all who went in by 'young Josep Riddaway', and Percy Stevins, telling Jan all about it, says in parenthesis, ' "Leery Jo," us calls 'en, 'cus he'm alwis hungered; and they say he id'n exac'ly, but I'm jiggered if he ab'm got a answer fer everybody.'

Coles remarked on the Devonians' use of 'd' for 'th'—as in 'droo,' 'datch,' 'dissles' or 'dashels', 'furder' and the like. This had the same sanction:

And if the weder stormy were
For cold she should have deyed there.

'Fader' and 'moder' occured frequently throughout the poems.

What about 'deyed'? There was, said Coles, no doubt how Chaucer pronounced it:

But e'er she deyed
Full piteously to God she preyde.

He recalled a gravestone, in the Bovey Tracey churchyard, to the memory of a man who 'dayed' on a certain date. He insisted that in many instances the old-fashioned Devonian insisted on sticking to the correct pronunciation.

And shod he was with great maistrie,
With shoon decoped.

'Shoon and hosen', he said, was still heard in North Devon—and he much preferred it to 'boots and stockings'. He commented, truly enough, that in most instances it was the more musical form which the rustic had retained, while the 'educative' person had adopted something much less melodious. He defied anyone to make 'you are' sound as sweet as 'you'm'.

He said that Jan went home of an evening to 'harken-in' to the wireless; he always bid one 'harken'—not 'listen'. Again, said his creator, he had good authority:

I stood full oft and long harkening
If that I heard a wight coming.
Alone I went in my playing
The small fowl's harkning.

'And what,' asked Coles, 'about "woodwalls" for "woodpeckers"? Old Jan always calls them "codwalls". I really begin to think that if Chaucer came back to life he would find himself more at home at Widecombe-in-the-Moor than in the drawing room of Mayfair.'

A. J. Coles was an expert. His only 'fault' was a complete lack of dullness. He was a born teacher.

SIX

Playwright, Actor, Editor

What the precise row was which led to his precipitate action, I do not know; but Coles left the little town of Bovey Tracey with considerable regret and in a fit of temper. The year was 1908, when party political feeling was running very high. One of the talents which he exercised in those days was in the rough-and-ready field of the hustings—and the particular hue of his many-coloured coat on this occasion was blue. Bovey Tracey in those days was intensely radical, and the unexpected victory in the then Mid-Devon division of Captain E. F. Morrison-Bell over the Liberal candidate, Mr. C. Roden Buxton, came as a staggering blow to many of the stalwarts. (This was a by-election two years before a general election.) It was well known that A. J. Coles had done much speaking and writing for the Tories in the division, though never in Bovey Tracey itself, and from the moment of the declaration of the poll his previously harmonious relations with a number of the folk became severely strained. Today it is difficult to realise just how bitter some political enmities were allowed to become during that post-election period. Whatever the cause, the social atmosphere seemed to be altered for the worse, and he resigned.

But it was at Bovey Tracey that the dramatic side of his career, both as playwright and actor, developed. Evening continuation classes, commonly known as 'night school', were held twice a week, and proved so successful that he worked in a third 'off-the-record' evening devoted to subjects not in the official curriculum—social, music, literary, dramatic, and so on. The interest shown was such that he decided to write a play for the students.

The play was called *Revel Day*, with a libretto written around Baring-Gould's *Songs of the West*. It was a colourful production, with hunting squire and dame, a son of marriageable age for hero, gentlemen and ladies of the hunt, two comic old men (Jan Gay and Job Craiker), milkmaids, ploughboys and gossips. The performers were all amateurs in the best sense of the word—the literal sense, of 'lovers'. Chesterton said, in defence of the amateur, that a thing that was worth doing was worth doing badly; but these sons and daughters of farmers, workers at the local pottery, schoolteachers, gardeners, shopkeepers and housekeepers—numbering over forty—did so well as almost to deserve the epithet 'professional'. The action of the play took place in the days of lace and fichus, panniers and poké-bonnets, buckles and bows: all the costumes were home-made; and Jack Furler, a friend from Newton Abbot, raised a small but efficient orchestra. Bovey Tracey Town Hall was packed that spring evening of 1907, and the audience included Baring-Gould who came from Lew Trenchard at no small inconvenience. At the end of the performance he spoke for ten minutes, and said, 'I came expecting the usual village concert, and instead we are witnessing a performance worthy of any large town.' When the curtain had fallen, he turned to the author and said, 'Mr Coles, this must not stop here. You must take it further afield.'

They did. In 1910 it provided evening entertainment for the Devon County Show at Newton Abbot. Billed for two nights, it packed the Alexandra Hall for four, and would have continued for six had the building not been booked for other purposes. The proprietor of Torquay's Theatre Royal saw the performance and invited them to take it lock, stock and barrel for a week to his theatre. After this it played for a week at the Theatre Royal in Exeter, and then went back to Torquay again.

During the first week of the play's Torquay performance A. J. C. took an opportunity afforded by his not being on stage to view part of the action. There were heavy plush curtains at the back of the circle, with space to walk behind, so he slipped out through the pass door, crept up the stairs to the circle, and got a view of the stage by peering through the curtains. The 'Saucy Ploughboy' song and the attractive dance of the milkmaids and ploughboys kept his eyes riveted on the stage. Soon the dancers exited amid chatter and laughter, leaving one actor alone in the centre. It was the tenor, dressed in hunting-pink. He was an actor thoroughly at home on the stage; but on this occasion he looked unhappy, glancing right and left and nervously tapping his top-boots with his hunting-crop. 'Why doesn't the prompter give him his line?' thought the author. 'Why doesn't he gag?' Then with horror, he suddenly realised that he himself was due on stage at that point. He dived for the door of the circle and took the stairs two at a time. But he was in hunting rig and overlooked his spurs: one of them caught in the carpet and the rest of the descent was a series of somersaults. Picking himself up at the bottom, he burst through the pass door, scattering milkmaids and villagers in all directions, dashed into the wings, and appeared on the wrong side just as the tenor, giving it up for a bad job, was coming off. In what was intended to be a hoarse whisper, but in fact went right through the house, he muttered, 'You damn fool.' It got the biggest laugh of the evening.

In 1922, a slightly revised version of *Revel Day* was put on at Torquay Pavilion, and Jack Furler wrote a new orchestration for this production. There were good press notices, one going so far as to say 'the production, acting, singing and dances will bear comparison with most visiting professional companies.' But its creator's greatest satisfaction came from the reflection that it all grew out of that rural night school.

It also grew out of his boyishness of spirit and dramatic instinct, shared in no small degree by his family. One summer, in their Torquay days, they formed a concert party for part of which they dressed in pierrot costumes. The programme consisted of songs, sketches, choruses and Jan Stewer monologues; and with it they toured parts of Devon with great success (and, among themselves, great hilarity). Harry found himself rehearsing for the concert party when he should have been studying for the law, although this did not prevent him later from establishing a successful solicitor's practice.

For the duration of the tours, the whole family rented rooms in Barnstaple. The company comprised A. J. Coles, Harry, Colin, Mary and Joan, and a young woman pianist. His wife never appeared on stage, but her work behind the scenes was indispensable. Miles of material were machined together to make curtains which could be fitted up in village halls as a back-cloth. Costumes were created: three outfits for the men, complete with traditional pom-poms and back frills in dark purple sateen; and for the ladies, dresses with purple underskirts of ballet net. Every night for months beforehand they rehearsed late at night, and finally the six of them set off with stage curtains, clothes and properties piled into 'Ole Biskit' while Harry rode on a 'Wolf' motor bike with solid tyres and a bell. They did one-night stands at Woolacombe, Torrington, Westward Ho!, Croyde Bay and Braunton.

A. J. Coles wrote a number of plays, one of which (*Barnet's Folly*) had a successful West-End production. *The Cat and Pigeons* was a light-hearted comedy with a slight inner seriousness and a double meaning in its title—the name of the hotel in which it was set, and the familiar proverb. Reading it, the author's role of Major Freddie Cartoosh seems a minor one. Seeing him in the part (I saw it at Exeter's Theatre Royal after the Second World War) he came over as a wryly amused observer of the other characters' pomposities and vitriolic talkativeness: he said little, but quizzically looked on and dryly summed up the human situation. In a way, Major Cartoosh was a spruced-up Jan, commenting (like him) upon the follies and frailties of mankind—much as Chaplin's *Monsieur Verdoux* was the immortal tramp in a smarter guise. *The Cat and Pigeons* was put on in the Barnfield Hall, Exeter, in 1938 by the Grendon Players. (This group was named after the Grendon Hotel in Exeter, which Coles ran—or more accurately, his wife and daughters ran, while his restless nature was engaged elsewhere—from 1934 until the middle of the war.) A local report referred to the merits of the actors in this performance, adding, 'Others who share in the success of the play are Joan St Ewer and Harry Coles.' It was licensed 'on the understanding that the following omission will be made. Act I, page 7, "and his shop window half full of contraceptives".'

The Grendon Players also put on his *Mr Furlinger*. Incidentally, as in other productions, the stage manager was Mr J. S. Bowey and the assistant stage manager Miss Mary Coles, who later became man and wife. This play was a deliberate, quite conscious attempt by A. J. Coles to emulate Ralph Lynn: he went to some pains to get his mouth and teeth to look like Lynn's, and wore the familiar monocle. The dialogue he gave himself was also modelled on that which Ben Travers gave Lynn—footling and foolish—as the apparently silly ass stumbled over his words and, in trying to extricate himself, became increasingly involved. It is an ingenious tale that holds the attention in reading (I never saw it performed) even if its dialogue does not have the persistent sparkle of the best of the Aldwych farces. Perhaps its main interest today lies in the stangely prophetic stage direction that 'the action of the play takes place at the house of Belarius Collandine, scientific engineer and inventor, discoverer of a device for enabling an aeroplane to hover stationary in the air and travel at the slowest speed.' From this book's point of view, it is another example of the man's remarkable readiness to turn his hand to so many forms of writing and acting.

Agatha's Heaven is as different from the other two plays as they are from each other. It is not a dialect play, nor is it specifically set in Devonshire; but its characters are truer to life, and more clearly based on types known to its writer. Its continuing popularity with repertory companies has been due to the intrinsic sweetness of the tale, which revolves around a maiden lady's attempt to turn her residence, the Old Rectory, into a thriving tea garden and, eventually, a hotel. However, romance was never Coles's strong point. As Mary put it: 'My father could never write nor produce a love scene. I produced a play he had been in, Delderfield's *Follow the Plough*, and he congratulated me on finding two young people who could do it . . . I thought, "Yes, that's because I taught them how to make love." '

Its first production at the Barnfield, produced by the author's son Colin and with his daughter taking the strenuous role of Agatha Cunningham, coincided with the London premiere of his one outstanding play. This was *Barnet's Folly*, which had begun as a modest one-acter and ended as a full-length West-End success. It had, in fact, about a hundred performances in the Haymarket Theatre in 1935, and deserved a much longer run. It was written in the late 1920s, when Coles was trying to scratch out a living on

5. Scene from *Barnet's Folly* at the Theatre Royal, Haymarket (Muriel Aked and A. J. Coles).

6. Jan Stewer in 'Ole Biskit'
7. A. J. Coles in the film *All Along, Down Along*

Five Mile Farm, in the Whitestone parish near Exeter. This was a period of depression on the land, and it seemed to him that there was need for more active co-operation among farmers. It seemed to him inevitable that certain types of people (represented in this play by William Burridge), from a distrust of others and a selfish regard for themselves, would always knock the bottom out of any real attempts at co-operation. It was out of this experience that *Barnet's Folly* was created. In an inspired moment he sent the script to Bernard Copping, producer of the Plymouth Repertory Players; and notices duly appeared in the local press saying it would be presented by them at the Plymouth Repertory Theatre on Monday 10 August 1931, for six nights and a matinee. Coles took good care that all his friends and acquaintances saw the advertisements. He even showed it to the man who came for the rabbits—though he rather missed the point and asked if it was any good for the rheumatics.

Coles was not a hardened first-nighter. He sat through the first performance of *Barnet's Folly* in a sort of trance, and in such a state of nerves that, as he said afterwards, he feared the people near him would suspect him of being a fugitive from justice. He later excused himself by saying that he was always a somewhat introspective sort of person and inclined to be shy, which I think was true. It was a good company, and the play was well received. The part of George Growsell, which the author was later to make so markedly his own, was played by Leslie Sanders.

About a year later A. J. Coles received a letter from Chloe Gibson (then of Torquay, but later associated with several London theatrical successes) asking if she might produce *Barnet's Folly* with her own company at Torquay Pavilion and if he himself would play the part of George Growsell opposite her Hannah Mudge. This production ran for a week and was seen by the manager of Exeter's Theatre Royal, Percy Dunsford, with the result that it was put on at Exeter. There its first two performances were seen by Roy Limbert of the Malvern Company who, after the second, undertook to put it on in London's West End within a specified time. It took nearly three years to get there, meanwhile being tried out in a few chosen theatres with the Malvern Company—Coles always playing the part of Growsell—and by the Birmingham Repertory in the Pier Pavilion, Eastbourne, where its reception encouraged Sir Harry Jackson to bring it to town.

Horace Watson had agreed to present *Barnet's Folly* at the Haymarket when his existing commitments had expired. When that would be he found it impossible to say, as it would depend upon the length of runs of the plays already accepted, but he was absolutely opposed to giving the part of George Growsell to 'Jan Stewer', of whom he had never heard. (Coles said he probably thought Jan was a Dutchman.) To present a play by an unknown writer was one thing, but to put in the lead a man who had only recently graduated from the amateur ranks, and had had little previous experience in any of the better-known theatres and none whatever in London, was quite another. However, Roy Limbert was quite convinced that 'Jan' was the inevitable choice for the part, and here showed great percipience. Finally Watson said he would put the matter to an independent arbitrator and accept his decision. This was the distinguished producer of the day, H. K. Ayliff, who had been commissioned to produce the play when it was put on at the Haymarket. The play was due for a fairly long season in Jersey, so Ayliff went there to see it and reported in favour of the author playing Growsell.

There were several—mostly minor—alterations to the original script. The new version was the one produced at the Theatre Royal, Exeter, with Chloe Gibson playing Hannah Mudge, the author George Growsell, and Phyllis Calvert the part of Nellie Lannacott ('about twenty-two, attractive both in appearance and manner'). The part of Richard Barnet was played by Ralph Michael. The Birmingham Rep. production was in the autumn of 1934; and *Barnet's Folly* was put on at the Haymarket by Roy Limbert on 14 February 1935, with Chloe Gibson now playing the small part of a neighbour. Coles was again Growsell, Muriel Aked was Hannah Mudge, Ralph Michael this time was Sam Burridge, Mary Jerrold Mrs Lannacott, May Agate Mrs Burridge, and Herbert Lomas, Mark Lannacott.

Two major changes were also made for the Haymarket version. One concerned costume. When Ayliff saw Coles with the Jan Stewer wig, he said, 'What on earth's that?' 'Part of my make-up.' 'What, with your lovely cranium? Take it off.' As George Growsell, Coles wore a moustache instead of the ear-to-ear beard, and no wig; but he reverted to the wig and whiskers for all his subsequent Jan Stewer performances—when he made up at all. Growsell was really Jan in another guise. The bits of 'business' he introduced, such as an unsuccessful attempt to roll up a piece of carpet, grumbling, 'It's follerin' me 'bout' (not in the script) are pure Jan Stewer. So is the following piece of dialogue, from the same part of the play, where Growsell and Hannah are sadly preparing the farmhouse for the impending sale:

HANNAH. Put them chairs back in their places. Master'll be in in a minute, and there's no sense in having the place looking like a Troy Town, reminding everybody of what's coming off. (*She goes L.*) Take them chairs out where they belong. (*He turns the chair up and the seat falls out.*) Mind, that comes out.

GEORGE. Who told you? (*The end of the next chair comes out in his hand.*) Does this one come out too?

At the London production I had the sense that I was the only person in the Haymarket who laughed out loud at this exchange. In a post-war Exeter production the whole audience laughed. Perhaps this form of comedy is essentially west-country.

The second major change was the final curtain. In the original script the two comedy characters, Hannah and George, left the scene for good about three-quarters of the way through the last act and were thus off-stage for Richard Barnet's dramatic disclosure to the Lannacott family of his father's culpability, and the ultimate reconciliation of the two young lovers. The original version had ended with Richard saying 'Good-bye' and going to the door. Nellie says 'Dick', and the final stage directions were:

(*He turns towards her. NELLIE holds out her arms and RICHARD goes to her. The curtain falls as they embrace.*)

Ayliff asked for the two comics to be kept on-stage, and George Growsell to have the final word. Coles must have rewritten it, and it is a vast improvement. The Lannacotts invite Richard for a meal. He says, 'But I thought that you—I thought—' He looks bewildered. Nellie asks, 'Hadn't you better think again?' They embrace, and George says to Hannah, 'That's what you've got to do to me—see?'

The second-act curtain is equally effective. 'Barnet's Folly' was the contemptuous name given to the scheme for co-operative distribution of local farm produce—and the plot centres around the attempts of William Burridge and his wife to marry their children off to the best advantage. 'Put your shoulders straight, 'Et', Mrs Burridge constantly says to her daughter Hettie, who, at the play's outset, is never allowed to speak for herself. This defeats Barnet's scheme, which results in the Lannacotts having to face bankruptcy. George Growsell and Hannah Mudge are given kindly notice by their employer. Hannah says, 'If anybody wants me to get out of this house they'll have to turn me out', and quickly leaves the stage. George, rising and stolidly turning to Mark Lannacott, repeats a question he has been asking intermittently throughout the act: 'Have I got to send they steers to market tomorrow, Master, or no?'

Coles later called the final curtain on that first night at the Haymarket, with its repeated calls of 'Author!', the greatest moment of his life. He had written the play for his own amusement, with no idea of its ever being performed in London and most of the principal provincial towns. Of Devon peasant stock himself, he had lived the greater part of his life among the sort of people he wrote about. George Growsell, the part he played several hundred times, was based on characters he had met over and over again, with different names but always with the same dry wit and crusted loyalty. The mean-spirited Burridges and the open-hearted Lannacotts he also knew well—and he had met scores of Hannah Mudges.

Although primarily a comedy, the play, as already described had a serious inner theme. Although it was written in Devon its chief problem was universal, and Coles was gratified to find that it was received as well in the north and the midlands as in the south. He could not go wrong with this one. It was made into a radio and television play. It is, in my view, a better and less-contrived play than Eden Phillpott's better known *The Farmer's Wife*, which is in the same genre. Coles did, in fact, play Churdles Ash in that play—and should, in my opinion, have been given the part in the film version instead of Wilfrid Lawson (who scored a huge success in *Pygmalion* as Eliza Doolittle's dustman father, but was here hopelessly miscast). Both men played the part of Churdles Ash on radio. It need not be stated which gave it the true west-country flavour. It is even probable that Coles's interpretation was a more authentic one than that of Cedric Hardwicke—who once remarked to the former, 'You know that I can *act* Churdles Ash, because you've seen me—but you *were* George Growsell.' George Growsell, grumbling at the invention of Summertime—'twenty past five according to the Gover'ment and twenty past four according to the Almighty. And the Gover'ment knows better than the Almighty as usual'—was an authentic characterisation.

Some highbrow critics adopted a condescending attitude towards this homely, simple, sentimental melodrama, and some objections were raised to the intrusion into the West End of a play written and acted by a virtual amateur; but the audiences loved it. Some of the critics went astray as to its precise location: the *News Chronicle* said its setting was Dorset, the *Daily Herald* prevaricated with Wessex, and the *Morning Post* even more cautiously said it was the west country. Most of the others correctly said Devon—it was left to the *Evening Standard* to describe it as 'a lovable play of the Cotswolds'.

By 30 November 1935, its author was able to write that *Barnet's Folly* had played in Malvern, Birmingham, Bognor, Folkestone, Eastbourne, Torquay, Exeter, Wimbledon, Hammersmith, Stratford, Sheffield, Newcastle, Bournemouth, and Oxford—and was due to play at Manchester and Wolverhampton. Its amateur performances from November 1936 to January 1950 had nearly 380 first nights, almost entirely in different cities, towns and villages of the land. The first of these was at Hull, the last at St Anne's; and in between (scanning the carefully preserved list at random) it was shown by amateur companies at Manchester, Reading, Pinner,

Windermere, Wigan, Llandrindod Wells, Aberfan, Bedford, Southport, Liverpool and Rochdale. There were critics who said that this rustic comi-tragedy might appeal well enough to west-country audiences but would fail elsewhere, while others said precisely the reverse. Both were overwhelmingly disproved. There is also still in existence a list (from 1937 to 1949) of thirty-four repertory lettings and two broadcasts.

The April 1935 issue of *Play Pictorial*—a glossy magazine devoted to the theatre and incorporating *The Play*, *The Play Souvenir* and *Plays and Players*—carried an impressive six-page spread on *Barnet's Folly*, with eleven photographs of scenes from the Haymarket production. There was a full outline of the plot, and a brief, highly favourable critique of the play beginning, 'This delightful play of West country life is splendidly acted. Its rich humour arises naturally from the characters and the situations and has nothing forced about it.' George Growsell was aptly described as 'a model of intractability'. The *Illustrated Sporting and Dramatic News* for Friday 15 April 1935, had a page of cartoons of the play's characters as seen by 'Nerman'. That of Jan as Growsell was perhaps the least lifelike of all—he would have been easier to caricature wearing the beard and wig with which west-country audiences in particular had become so familiar. In it, he was shown enacting the unscripted piece where he tried to roll up a carpet in Lannacott's farm. The amusing sketch of Jan in this undignified position was somewhat wryly captioned 'Portrait of a Playwright.'

Coles's range was enormous. Stuart Keen, film exhibitor and producer, who died at the relatively early age of sixty on Christmas Day 1976, was first introduced to him when they were both fond of amateur dramatics and he was taken along to Coles's newly formed group, the '36 Club'. At that time Coles was producing, for a provincial drama league festival, one-act plays ranging from Chekhov to Sacha Guitry. Keen told me: 'As a producer of other authors' plays, his regard for detail and creation of "business" encouraged amateurs, and he got the last ounce out of their parts through his utmost thoroughness. He could transform a play in an evening's rehearsal.' Keen spoke of the outstanding performances given by Coles, such as in the role of the old judge in Elmer Rice's *Judgment* (based on the Reichstag fire in Hitler's Germany) when, pleading for mercy, he brought tears to the eyes of the audience at Exeter University. Coles's group came top in the drama league towards the end of the Second World War. He played the centenarian in *A Hundred Years Old*, a charming play about a Spanish family by the Quintero brothers. He was an amateur in the best sense of the word, and had he given less time to fellow amateurs he would undoubtedly have furthered his own career to greater financial advantage. Too generous with his time, he was taken advantage of. Nothing was too much trouble if it interested him, and he would work for unlimited periods of time in order to achieve satisfaction with any project.

Like other lovers of the drama, he haunted the Malvern Festival. There he once sat entranced as he listened to a handsome young man giving one of Shaw's characteristically long speeches as Dunois in *Saint Joan*. Afterwards he met the young man in Malvern Park, and plucked up courage to say, 'I think the day will come when I shall be proud to have met you.' The prophecy came true. The young man was Robert Donat.

At a meeting of the West Country Writers' Association at Bath, where there was much talk of Beau Nash, he commented: 'Down our way, bone ash is what us puts on the ground.'

It had long been Stuart Keen's ambition to make a short film in the west country which somehow had a place for Jan in it. A good deal of time was spent considering subjects, even including a visual treatment of the cricket-match monologue. Instead it was decided to make a travelogue which would capture the genuine atmosphere of Dartmoor and the parts the two men loved, as distinct from the pseudo-west-country Wardour Street impression. Coles was the obvious choice for the narrator, and, as Keen said:

It was not just a case of shooting the film and asking him to add a commentary. He remained with the film from the start, which included days and days of trailing. He was fresher at the end than the two younger men, Keith Gibb, the cameraman, (who also died in 1976) and myself. The film was taken up by the Rank Organisation to whom I made over the rights for five years, after which they withdrew it from their circulation. The film would have been nothing without Jan. *The 16mm Film Guide* reviewed it, and said this was a quality travelogue with a superb commentary "in the vernacular".

The film, *All Along, Down Along*, is a journey through the land of the Dart from its headwaters near Cranmere Pool in the heart of the moor to Postbridge, Grimspound, Wistman's Wood and Dartmeet. The journey continues through Buckland-in-the-Moor, Holne, Ashburton, Buckfastleigh (where work at the quarries is seen) and Totnes, to the beautiful English Rhine and the famous and historic harbour of Dartmouth. There are beautiful shots of the river at all stages of its growth, from a mere trickle among the lonely wastes and peat-bogs high up on Dartmoor to its calm estuary at Dartmouth. There are charming studies of wildlife of all kinds, especially the ponies, with an exciting and skilful round-up. This amateur production, dedicated to all lovers of Devon, lasts for about forty-five minutes, and was released in the autumn of 1951. A. J. Coles, whose voice is heard throughout, appears first at the film's outset.

Looking more like George Growsell than Jan Stewer, he walks up to the approaching car in a Devon country road, and says:

Aw, gude arternune. Was you lookin' for zomeone? Aw, you want to know the way? The River Dart? Oh, that's away out auver, ooh—what part of the Dart did you want? Oh, the *whole* of it? Oh, wull then, you want to find Dart 'Aid. I shude go to Fernworthy if I was you, that's a gude place to start from. That's right out over that country there, zee, oh as far as you can zee. You go, let me zee now, you, ah, you carry on along yer, and then you bend around a bit, and then you go, ah, let's zee, up over a bit of a nap, and then you go down over t'other zide, and then you carry on and bend around, and then you go, oh, let me zee, you go on, er, oh, a bit further then you'd think, and then—eh?—oh, you wants to get to Grimspound on the way? Oh, that's another matter. Wull, I wude'n go that way then. You want the Moreton road, yes, the Moreton road; ah, that's—you know the Moreton road? Aw, you don't? Aw, wull you carry on yer and turn on yer right and then you go on for a bit til you come to three roads, zee, you come to three roads, like this there (he demonstrates with his fingers) ah—wull, when you come to they three roads, zee, there's one gwain up there, and there's one gwain along there, and one that way. Wull, you don't take no account of 'ee, and you don't pay no attention to 'ee, you don't bother 'bout they two, zee, you carries along of 'ee, and then you go, oh, you goes on, let me zee—I cude go there, zee, but it's difficult to derect anybody else the way. What? Me go with 'ee? Aw, haw haw, giddout! Caw, darn my rigs, you've zaid something now, I'm danged if you ab'm. Wull, 'twude be very nice. Ah—let me zee, now 'tid'n market day. Aw, wull, I think I could manage you. Yes. Of course, Mother'll want to know who's doin' my work while I'm gallivantin' away. Now, let me zee. Jim can carry on with the dung-spreading, gude; George cude do the sheep, aye, there's naught that matters very much, I dont think. Caw! 'Twude be a gude idea. Aw, ha ha ha! Right, Wull, I'll go along with 'ee. Yes. Wull, you'll 'ave to start pretty early in the mornin', mind, 'cus us got to go all along, down along, and you'll pick me up yer, will 'ee? Aye! Yes. Wull, I'll be stood yer, zee, and you'll pick me up yer. Right. That's a bargain. Now mind, you'll have to get up bevore you goes anywhere. Goodbye. Goodbye to 'ee. Aw, my dear zaul, what 'ave I done fer myself now? Caw! . . . Yer! Come back! Aw, too late. Aw, I'm properly in fer it now.

The introductory words of this monologue were the ones he used in many 'how to get there' stories, of which the prototype, which he may well have originated, ends, 'If I was gwain to Nuton Abbot, I shude'n start from yer.'

In 1954 Coles provided the commentary for a film about the Bath and West Show. In the late 1950s, when the Bicton Agricultural Club was commissioned by the Devon Education Committee to make a film (called *Gateway to Heaven*) he also provided an excellent commentary, although eyebrows were raised by some committee members because of its humorous nature. Made in colour, this film is now out of circulation. Said Stuart Keen: 'He never did a dud commentary.'

It would be impossible to apply the word 'dud' to anything Coles undertook. He had left teaching and gone in for entertainment on stage and page as a full-time profession; he took the media of radio and television more or less in his stride, the techniques of the latter coming in handy for Jan's endless tales, in which he referred to it, with a scorn not shared by his creator, as 'this-yer *Barnet's Folly* caper'. But his mind was so active and his talents so various that he could not entirely confine himself to the character of Jan Stewer, for which he will be chiefly remembered. He was the managing editor of the *Mid Devon Advertiser* and the *Torbay News* from 1909 to 1913. And in between creating one immortal character and whole villages and parishes, he lightly found time off to play Toby Belch in *Twelfth Night* opposite Wendy Hiller as Viola and Walter Hudd as Malvolio—much as Shakespeare might have dashed off a couple of sonnets while engaged in the more serious business of writing *Hamlet*. He toured with CEMA (the Council for the Encouragement of Music and the Arts), a sort of highbrow version of ENSA.

All of these fields he deliberately set out to master. He did so without any specialised training, apart from the school of life, putting to the fullest use his keen observation of human nature. He had, for instance, no dramatic training as such, save that of trial and error. He never went to RADA, though he acknowledged the help given him by professional actors; he seemed to know all the tricks of the trade by sheer instinct. He might have become an advanced educationalist (though his strong strain of Victorianism would have saved him from some of the excesses of the libertarian schools), he could have become famous as a writer or producer of plays, and he had it in him to be at the very least a nationally known character-actor, if not a full-time member of the Royal Shakespeare Company. He toyed with this and that, but his mind was too active and his nature too procrastinating to settle down for long in any one of the media in which, for relatively short spurts, his talent briefly but brilliantly shone. If he had been a more disciplined man—which he was far from being—and concentrated on any single one of them, he would have conquered in the field of his choice. But in none of them, in such an event, would he have achieved immortality, and we should all have been the losers.

A. J. Coles tried (by no means without success) to become a playwright, but Jan gently restrained him. He said once that if he had his time over again, he would be an actor; Jan nodded his head sadly and sagely. He thought he would try his hand at being Ralph Lynn; but Jan said, 'Come yer!' Coles could not resist the peremptoriness of that call.

The word 'genius' is one to be used sparingly. A. J. Coles had many talents but in one thing only was he a genius. That, of course, was the creation of Jan Stewer. And that—at any rate in the first instance—he did not seek out, did not concentrate on, had no intention of making specially his own. Almost accidentally, he stumbled upon Jan Stewer—the first newspaper contribution thus signed was an editor's idea, not his own, the choice of a pseudonym being a quick, last-minute decision. Gradually, imperceptibly, Jan took over: for indeed it is almost as though Jan Stewer mastered Coles, rather than the reverse. What emerged was a composite character, yet an essentially unique one. There is a sense in which A. J. Coles was possessed—beneficently possessed—by a good demon, a kindly demon, a mirth-provoking demon, above all a Devonshire demon. And when Albert John Coles walked down Exeter High Street, it was only in one way that he was greeted by his many friends, 'Hello Jan.'

SEVEN

The Later Writings

During the 1920s, a leading Torquay bookseller suggested to A. J. Coles that he try a London publisher with a book. The result was *In Chimley Corner*, published by Herbert Jenkins in 1928 and the first of the revised reprints (though the rewriting in some instances virtually amounted to entirely fresh material). Some of the stories have been transformed almost out of all recognition—and if we no longer have quite the same sense of leisure and ignorance of the wider world (say anywhere above Somerset, which ranked as 'furrin' parts' along with anywhere overseas) that prevailed in many a Devon village before the First World War, this book is deservedly everybody's favourite.

The bookseller's suggestion presented Coles with the kind of challenge he could never resist, and a few weeks later, having to go to London on other business, he slipped the manuscript of *In Chimley Corner* into his bag. The next morning he went to York Street, but when he was in sight of the publishers he passed on the other side of the road and walked round St James's Square. Then he went back to look at the bright array of volumes in their gaily coloured jackets in the window; his behavior became increasingly like that of Charlie Chaplin in *Easy Street* as he passed and repassed the police station before at last madly rushing in to enlist. Coles hurried back into Piccadilly. It would be best, perhaps, to post the manuscript, or push it through the letter-box . . . but the letter-box wasn't big enough. Or perhaps he should take it in, drop it on the counter and run away . . . but suppose there wasn't a counter?

Finally Coles took a long breath, opened the door, and went in. The room was empty, and he was on the point of creeping out again when a clerk slid up a trap, with a snap that made him jump, and through the hatch inquired his business. He muttered something about the manuscript, and was invited to sit down. The clerk spoke into a phone, and invited Coles to follow him, saying one of the directors would see him. He was received by one John Grimsdick. They talked about Devon, and at last the manuscript was unwrapped along with the other little publications. The director looked through them, and said that they would publish the new book, adding there would be an initial payment of £50 on the day of publication. Then he invited the author out to lunch the next day. Grimsdick, it transpired, knew all about the Jan Stewer stories, greatly enjoyed them and, in fact, possessed some himself.

In Chimley Corner has a delightful introduction which laments the replacement of the open hearth by an American range. It also points out that the stories are not mere reprints but have all been rewritten, and Coles makes it clear that in his opinion they have thereby been considerably improved. This is an opinion with which at least one other person entirely concurs. There are many examples, but the prime one is the metamorphosis of the best (in my judgment) of the monologues. It began as 'Mrs Snell and the Census Paper', and ends as 'Jan and the Census Paper', without a mention of Mrs Snell. There is no comparison: the Mrs Snell version is a rough sketch, no more; the Jan version is a riot from start to finish. But the earlier version—and this also applies to several of the *Carrier's Van* pieces—offers the reader fascination and the privilege of seeing the first draft of a masterpiece. One of them has a story called 'The Swell Dinner'. This is an entirely different tale to the one of the same name in *In Chimley Corner*, which derives from 'The Hunt Dinner.' *In Chimley Corner* ends with a poem, 'The Song of the Settle', which illustrates A. J. C.'s skill as a versifier—to say 'poet' would be to use too strong a word. It teeters on the edge of sentimentality, but never tips over. The old-fashioned settle (a high wood-backed seat) tells of families it has seen come, grow up and go, and the penultimate verse is a most affecting description of what is clearly the settle's view of coffins coming into the room over the years. It is pathos which just stops short of bathos. Coles pulls it off in this instance, but, by and large poetry was not his strong line. For example, *In Chimley Corner* also contains a ballad, 'The Haughty Maid', whose meaningless and folksy chorus is exactly the sort of 'Mummerzet' which lends itself all too easily to parody by comedians such as Peter Sellers.

This book contains, more than most others, tales suited to monologue treatment. 'Jan's Fiddle' is the one story he tells of his earlier days: when Jan goes to buy the instrument, he is surprised to learn that the older they are the more money they are likely to cost. So he asks to be shown a 'colt'! He later drives his friends and neighbours mad with his playing, not having had a single lesson.

'The Swell Dinner' is still a firm favourite which is performed at all sorts of public functions and church social gatherings, and has been much plagiarised.

'Jan and the Census Paper' is the best piece for public performances, containing as it does almost literally a laugh a minute. As I have already mentioned, Coles polished this one from the original *Carrier's Van* series into a perfect little gem. After all these years—my own copy of *In Chimley Corner* is from the fifth printing, which brought the total to 21,481 copies—it is still capable, if performed with any sense of timing at all, of reducing an audience to almost helpless mirth. Today there is rising in the west country a generation that did not know Jan, and it is refreshing to hear the unashamed laughter of the most sophisticated teenagers who are listening to it for the first time.

'Our Electric Light Scheme' must have been an anachronism almost as soon as it was written, but it is still delightful both to read and hear. Much play is made of the simple villagers' misunderstanding of 'currents'. For example, told that the 'currant' runs along the wire, Mrs Endycott comments that they must be a terribly small sort—not unlike those kept by Mrs Coombs in her shop. Mrs Porter adds that, to make matters worse, Mrs Coombs is asking tenpence halfpenny a pound for them. Lias Buzzacott deliberately misunderstands the reference to 'buttons', by which is meant electric switches, and expatiates, with true Devon eloquence, on their nuisance element. He illustrates by explaining that he had bent down to pick up his pipe from the floor. The result? He had only one button left to go home with. He also expands upon the calamity that would ensure if he dropped his pipe again—as far as he is concerned, buttons are anathema. He would take an entirely different view of the matter if the trick could be pulled off with a safety pin or a bit of cord, but he makes it abundantly clear that if it *has* to be done with buttons, he will stolidly refuse to vote for it. Ever-conservative, so does Muddlecombe, and the electric-light scheme falls through.

'Jan's Cricket Match' is firmly immortalised, in that to this day some Devon cricket teams call the sight screen the 'rin-jan'. At one point, when Jan and the parson are sharing the batting, Jan, on hearing the parson shouting at him to run, runs as fast as he can after the ball.

The above are the well-known stories, being those which Coles most frequently performed in public. He was the master of both quiet and broad humour, and to make a generalisation it may be said that the quietly humorous stories are the most readable and the broadly humorous ones the most actable.

I never heard A. J. Coles recite 'Will Brewer and the Boots', but many years ago heard someone else do so at a function in Bideford Market—then the venue for many public entertainments and political rallies—and it brought the house down. He gives, in dialect form, a vivid picture of Will Brewer, a man who just jogged along in his old-fashioned way, year in and

8. Poster for *Twelfth Night* at Coventry. 'Jan Stewer' appears among some very well-known stage names.

9. Jan Stewer

year out, and rarely went beyond the boundaries of his own parish. He said the responses when babies were christened, rang the chimes for folk to go to church while they were still alive, buried them in the ground when they had departed this life, and then tolled their souls to heaven. (There were times, Jan drily observes, when he had his doubts about the latter.) It is a perfect portrait of a simple, reliable, steady-going soul. But one day, sent to meet a lawyer in an Exeter hotel, Will Brewer finds himself thrust into a new and terrifying world. Each time he asks someone in the hotel if anyone has been inquiring for him, he is told to ask the Boots. The constant repetition of what, to him, conveys merely foot apparel drives him almost literally mad. On asking where the boots are, he is sent down some stairs into the suberranean depths of the hotel. And there they are, a whole row of boots before his startled eyes—boots of every shape, size and colour, lined up against the wall like a regiment of soldiers. The story is, if anything, rather more frightening than funny, for there is a nightmare atmosphere about this simple soul's mounting hysteria. He asks the boots if they have heard anyone asking for Will Brewer and, receiving no reply, he picks them up one at a time and inquires of each individually. Still receiving no reply, he flings each boot as far as he can, and soon the air seems full of boots flying in all directions. The whole hotel is roused by the noise and, told that the man wearing the green apron is the Boots, he sarcastically comments that he must be called that because he wears shoes.

What Coles so brilliantly reproduces with unflagging invention, is the countryman's constant amazement at the intrusion into his normally slow-moving environment of the unknown phenomena of an ever-changing world—be it the mysteries of the internal-combustion engine, swell dinners, posh parties or hot-water bottles (a new-fangled 'invention' compared with the more familiar warming-pan). Another phenomenon Jan explores with great effectiveness is that of the countryman's children moving, through marriage, to a higher station in life, and his discomfiture when visiting them. Jan Tremlett, visiting his married daughter, finds that a man does not lose the habits of sixty years in a fortnight. Their meal-time habits, late retirings and risings appal him, as do the ornaments. His daughter had, he relates, about a dozen little red devils standing on the mantelpiece in the sitting-room with their tongues poking out. These and several others he denounces as indecent and ugly; his daughter defends them as being 'novel'. He concludes that 'novel' means 'ugly', and Tom Salter's crushing comment is that Mr Tremlett is probably right. Tom himself recalls hearing the parson say once that Mrs Chamsey had her head full of novel ideas—and she, goodness only knew, was ugly enough.

'Higher Education' comes to Muddlecombe in the form of a series of lectures. Jan's malapropism is 'serious', which he considers a highly appropriate epithet. It seems all the wrong people go to the lectures, and Jan concludes that higher education is not what Muddlecome needs. What they really need is a bit of lower education, which might achieve something. This comes strangely from the writings of one who was, in his own day, a pioneer of teaching methods: it might be argued that this is Jan speaking, not Coles. It is always dangerous to attribute all of a character's sentiments and limitations to his creator. But here something of Coles undoubtedly did find expression in Jan, for although he was delineating the resistance to change with which as a teacher he himself had had to contend, his own impatience with novelty for novelty's sake also crept in. He would not have approved of the strangely named 'method' school of acting—he insisted on his fellow amateur actors taking the same pains he did himself to master his art. His teaching methods were ahead of their time, but he was a pioneer who yet saw the common sense of sticking to a few basic principles. And Jan, with his creator's acute perception, sees that it is the untutored who need the benefits of new knowledge, not the 'arty-crafty' types who, like the Athenians of St Paul's day, 'spent their time in nothing else, but either to tell, or to hear some new thing'. The Devonshire villages had (and still have) their full quota of such types; they were giving themselves airs and graces, and Coles, through Jan, slew them with a word.

There is a recurrent theme running through all the books, which is that the cobbler must stick to his last. It is summed up in the title of another very popular story, 'Every Man To His Trade', a tale in which the much-quoted Turney Gurney for once holds the field and tries his hand at running his brother-in-law's old fashioned grocer's shop. This relative is a type that is fast becoming obsolete. But not, happily, altogether; for here and there, in not a few isolated villages, he comes into his own, with his long white apron, his fingers spread out on the counter, and his ingratiating yet sincere inquiries after the health of the customer's wife or husband. The story is a period piece not only from the point of view of prevailing prices, but also as regards the style of shop, so outmoded in this, the day of the supermarket.

Turney Gurney is, of course, another Jan—if not Jan in disguise. Coles would sometimes, though infrequently, make a character other than Jan the central figure in a story; but more often than not he has, if not Jan's mannerisms, his insatiable curiosity when confronted with the novelty of the untried, his irresistible impulse to experiment, and his unbounding confidence that he can succeed as well as the expert. Turney Gurney observes how Ned serves all small quantities in a sort of bag, made by twisting some paper around his fingers, forming it into a point at one end and finally pinching it up to hold it together. He gets his chance to perform this feat when Ned is called away, is, of course, singularly inept, and before long chaos reigns. Everyone is shouting at once, especially one particularly obnoxious little boy who keeps on demanding treacle. Customers are calling for butter, candles, clothes-pegs, pepper—and treacle, treacle, treacle, which is soon in all its sticky evidence.

The next three books followed in quick succession. *A Parcel Of Ol' Crams* came out in 1930, with an entertaining Author's Note giving the various usages of the expression. A landlady uses it to describe her current residents who are food faddists, indeed vegetarians; a mother so describes her son's teacher's insistence upon his taking a tooth-brush to school so that he can clean his teeth three times a day; a labourer goes to a political meeting and employs the phrase to sum up his unfavourable impression of respective performances of the speakers. And so on. Should his (ie Jan's) neighbours ever see the collection of tales in the book it is to be assumed they would also use the dismissive expression, but he neatly forestalls them by using it as the book's very title. 'Crams' they may be, but the humour and psychological insights are unflagging. The phrase has an air of finality, though softer and less harsh to hear than the phrases for which it is a substitute, which are various. It can be used to dismiss the interference of a bureaucratic official who comes to inspect a farmer's 'place' and insists on the instalment of 'proper' floors for the cows, with gutters of a specified width and depth. As a definition it is unarguable, the last word: it means (though this is an inadequate translation) 'a pack of nonsense'.

'When Jan Played Football' is nearly as funny as the story of the cricket match, though more lacking in invention, and some people rate it as highly. It is almost the only piece in the book which Coles performed in public. I confessed my surprise to Harry Coles that his father never publicly used 'Speech on a Church Clock', one of the funniest and most brilliant sketches. Harry said this had been considered, but that his father abandoned the idea on the grounds that it was too static and lacked any real opportunities for the kind of acting his perfectionism demanded. Yet, as I have proved, it always goes down well with an audience; it is a perfect parody of that eloquence which says precisely nothing (like Peter Sellers's political speech).

Outstanding in this collection is 'Jan's Adventures in London', which is divided into four sections. In 'On the Underground', he becomes predictably confused by the tunnels, which he compares to a 'rabbut's berry'. Asking the way to Russell Square, he is told to change at Piccadilly Circus—and ruefully wishes he could change 'to' (into) a ferret in order to find his way out of these rabbit holes. 'The Resolving Staircase' refers of course, to the escalators. When Jan retails his experiences back in

Muddlecombe, Tom Salter observes that the process must use up a good many in a year, and Jan, who has been doing a bit of thinking, observes that they must have some means of using the same ones over again. At the Continental Hotel, Jan finds himself embarrassed by the idea of speaking to the young lady at the reception desk. Plucking up courage, he goes up to her and asks if he can stay there overnight. He assures her that he has brought his own night-shirt, a brush and comb, and all he requires—all he wants is a bed for the night. He also adds that his wife has impressed upon him that he is to be sure and ask if they would please see that it had been properly aired. Whereupon the girl laughs (for a second time), and it dawns upon Jan that she must have guessed he had come up from the country. The final miracle is the ever-opening door. In this section Jan is ashamed at not having risen until the late hour of eight o'clock for breakfast. He asks the Boots if all the breakfasts have been cleared, and cannot understand when the Boots points out that it is *only* eight o'clock. Then he asks the way to the kitchen—now it is the Boots' turn to be uncomprehending—for as far as Jan is concerned, the kitchen is the natural place to have one's breakfast.

These tales can still be enjoyed and laughed at even though they are now considerably out of date. Few folk, however rustic, would be surprised to find running hot water in the hotel bedroom, or react (as Jan does) to the waiter's swiftness in the story of 'The Swell Dinner'. But everything in this volume is vintage material. There is the hilarious story of the formation of Tom Tolley's band, where a good deal of fun is to be got out of the octave and the players' persistence in not stopping at 'C' but going up to 'W' or down to 'F' or 'Q'—and so on. The bandmaster, Tom Tolley is, however, delighted at this first attempt: after a bit of practice, he assures them they will be in tune. 'Or else in prison', observes Peter Sillage.

There is a nostalgic backward look in 'Tales from the Carrier's Cart' presented in this book as a four-part chapter. As in the carrier's-van portraits already referred to, there was much harmless badinage in those more leisurely days. There was more conversation; and if it was not always on the highest intellectual level, this loss was more than atoned for by its extremely homely and good-humoured nature. Jan regrets the speed brought about by the advent of the car—the old carrier's van will never return. Yet perhaps this is just as well, for the journeys in those days were slow, often very cold, and exceedingly tedious, especially if one was one in a hurry. But then, one wasn't always in a hurry.

When people said to Chesterton, 'You can't put the clock back', he would reply simply, 'You can'. This is not quite the trick answer it might at first appear to be, for what he meant was that if one desired to revert to a former moral or theological position, one could in fact do so as simply as if one moved the actual hands of a mantelpiece clock. It is, of course, impossible to get on to a sort of Wellsian time-machine and go back to those days, but Jan makes it possible to a certain degree by this nostalgic backward glance. This is the voice of the older A. J. Coles, looking back to his Puddington days and recapturing something of that more leisurely era—you can almost hear him sighing as he draws to the close of this reminiscence. The car, however, was to provide A. J. Coles with a wonderful source of adventures. It served his purpose—all things did, and had he been born a few decades later we should have missed some of the tales of the Boer War period but there can be no doubt that he would have made capital out of computers. The car, as will be seen, was a real one, but the tales Jan relates were the figments of his creator's imagination. It remains a matter for conjecture which were the more eventful adventures—those related in *Ole Biskit*, or the actual ones experienced by A. J. Coles in his own car.

It is not without significance that when Coles, in the later volumes, recalled those earlier and cosier carrier's-van days, he occasionally reverted, probably quite unconsciously, to the uncompromising form of dialect he employed in the original stories. Those days, after all, were the source of his inspiration.

'Tales from the Carrier's Cart' as it appeared in *A Parcel of Ol' Crams* was, as I have already mentioned, divided into a four-part chapter, and the titles are in each case sufficiently descriptive: 'A Parcel of Trumpery': 'Tom Zalter's Day's Pleasure' (a sardonic title, this, for Tom has suffered much from a day's outing in a car and returned with relief to his more familiar cart); 'Have We Lived Before?' (it's surprising what topics were raised in the carrier's van); and 'Breathing-Room Only'. This is the last chapter, and there is an air of finality in the words THE END. It is as though this memory of former days has blotted out both the past and the future. But A. J. Coles never succumbed to that common ingredient of old age, a useless hankering after the irretrievable past; he remained young in spirit to the end of his long life, adapting with remarkable facility to the ethos of each new era. He was always at ease in the company of those of a much younger generation.

This was not, of course, the end, for he had more to say yet, and more laughs up his sleeve. *Yap* followed in 1931. There is no sign of failing powers here, although 'The Singing Match'—a variant on the 'Tom Tolley's Band' theme—is not quite as funny as its predecessor. And the golf episode is the least effective (though longest) of the sporting triad. There is, however, much for which to be grateful. There is 'The Working Model' (about a waxworks show, and which goes back to Boer War days); and 'For the Good of the Cause', in which Jan allows himself (not without protest) to be made up as 'Enry Eight and is distracted by being unable to reach an itching spot of the padding used to make him rotund. There is 'The Likeness Taker' (camera); and 'Judgment', a delightful thumbnail sketch of Nathaniel Webber, a sanctimonious local preacher with a 'hell-fire' approach, a type now virtually extinct.

'The Wedding' tells the story of the marriage of Jan's daughter Jane—and is mildly humorous, with more than a fair share of sentiment thrown in. Sentiment and romance, as has been noted, were never Coles's strong points, and here a parallel may be drawn between Coles and Charles Dickens. (To many any comparison between the great Victorian novelist and one whose relatively obscure fame rests mainly on the writing of humorous stories in the Devonshire dialect will seem ludicrous. By way of excuse, I can only say that it is in the form of criticism in both cases, and that the resemblance is a valid one.) G. K. Chesterton writing about *The Pickwick Papers*, pointed out that Dickens's indirect and unintended pathos was far more effective than his deliberate attempts to arouse compassion. Oscar Wilde, it will be remembered, said that a man would have a heart of stone if he could read the death of Little Nell without laughing. In contrast to that, Chesterton quoted Tony Weller's words to his dying wife as he repeated them to his son: ' "Susan", I says, "you've been a wery good vife to me altogether: keep a good heart, my dear, and you'll live to see me punch that 'ere Stiggins's 'ead yet.' She smiled at this, Samivel . . . but she died arter all." ' Happily, Coles did not try his hand, so far as I know, at death-bed scenes. 'The Wedding' has Ann piping the inevitable tear—it is homely, and therefore acceptable, but in so far as it is an attempt to make us share, however lightly, Ann's tears, it fails. Henry James said he found more life in what was obscure and subject to interpretation than in 'the gross rattle of the foreground'. It is, indeed, part of Coles's genius that Ann's and Jan's mutual affection remains apparent throughout the Stewer saga, despite the fact that they seem to be perpetually throwing verbal brickbats at each other. That he succeeds in achieving this cannot be explained as a mere trick of the trade, for it is an atmosphere that pervades the whole.

'Lias in Town', though somewhat overshadowed in theme by the earlier and longer adventures of Jan in London, is short and sharp and has much to commend it. But usually the role of the innocent abroad was reserved for Jan. On this point, Chesterton's book on Dickens comes to my aid again: Pickwick, he says, is the greenhorn who is the ultimate victor in everything—he is, to use the expressive phrase, 'taken in', which is to see the inside of things. The greenhorn is taken in by life, whereas the sceptic is cast out by it. There is about the character and nature of Jan a certain childlike innocence. He is startled by all the wonders which an ever-changing world has to offer, and is sometimes critical of them, but he gets a good deal out of life. He is a superb raconteur; he is a happy man; he is not defeated by life's slings and arrows, but rises up again ready for the next emergency or adventure. He is like Felix, the cartoon cat of my youth, who was never permanently cast down but, whatever befell, kept on walking still . . .

Few parts of England can have been so startled by innovations as Jan Stewer country, and each novelty exceeds any previous one. When Percy Stevins tells Jan the story of Excombe's fancy-dress ball, it leaves in the shade all the nine-days' wonders he has ever witnessed in his native village. He recalls the elopement of young Donovan with Farmer Carter's daughter; he remembers a fire which destroyed one side of the street (two thatched cottages and a barn); and he 'brings to mind' Peter Daw going to jail for stealing money from the church collections, in spite of being the church warden. He has seen many other such weighty incidents, but the fancy-dress ball surpasses them all. They alway do. Every fresh experience is 'the greatest': cricket match, football match, singing match, jumble sale or fancy-dress ball—whatever it may be—beats cock-fighting (a phrase that has happily dropped from our vocabulary with the decease of the 'sport'). What Coles did, of course, was first create a richly comic but credible character who has all our sympathy—essentially an innocent when outside his well-trodden paths—and place him in an unfamiliar environment. There are a thousand possible variants on this theme, and Coles explored most of them.

Most of the contributions he made to the Devonshire press are, sadly lost utterly—unless there is to be found somewhere a Jan Stewer devotee who has kept them all. Some of these were continuous narratives, any of which would have made a fascinating book (I recall 'The Gurt Romance', which seemed to go on for ever).

The last of the great quartet of the dialect books was *Ole Biskit*, Coles's own favourite and arguably the best, though not from the point of view of recitation. (For the latter purpose, *In Chimley Corner* retains the greatest popularity.) It was probably his favourite in view of the fact that 'Ole Bisket' was a real car. Between the wars, Coles bought an ancient car, with much brass in its make-up which shone like burnished gold about twice a year, for a week each time. From what had obviously been its original colour (and still was in some places), it was promptly nicknamed 'Ole Biskit' by the Coles family. Ole Biskit was a 'tourer' with a hood and side-screens which, in the event of a sudden shower, could be rigged up and fixed in place, usually by about the time that the rain stopped. It was in Ole Bisket that A. J. Coles, sometimes alone and sometimes with members of his family, toured the countryside to outlying village halls as well as large towns, in days when motorways were merely a Wellsian dream.

There can be no doubt that Coles's own experiences in Ole Biskit provided a great source of inspiration for the incidents in *Ole Biskit*. Once he drove across Bodmin Moor, on a dark night and in a blinding snow storm. He had an open newspaper spread on his lap, and every mile or so he pulled up, got out of the car, emptied a pile of snow from the paper, scraped a peephole in the windscreen, and resumed the journey. There was no windscreen wiper, no spare wheel except a 'Stepney' (a tyred rim which, in the event of a puncture, was clamped on beside the existing wheel), no electric lighting (the headlights burned acetylene gas, and the side and tail lamps used plain oil and wick), no foot throttle, no self-starter (the starting-handle was a permanent feature), no front- and little rear-wheel braking. There was an engine and transmission, and not much else.

Yet Ole Biskit always got there and back eventually, even if he (Ole Biskit was always 'he', never 'it' and still less 'she') had to do it on three wheels and two cylinders. Or so Coles claimed in later life; but there was, as his son Harry told me years later, more than one exception. He was driving with Harry and his other son Colin to perform at Liskeard, when they had trouble with the propellor shaft. The universal joint behind the gearbox disintegrated and hung loose, just avoiding touching the road. Harry and Colin—who were always the mechanics in such situations, not their father—found the parts on the road and, using some equipment from the toolbox, put the pieces back and the three continued their journey. When they came to a garage at South Brent, the sons suggested that they have the problem dealt with there, in spite of their father's insistence that since they had got the car going they might as well carry on. He was overruled, and they had to leave the car at the garage and go on to Liskeard by taxi. Coles was reluctant, but the show had to go on and there was clearly no alternative. Ole Biskit was put to rights again, ready for the next adventure. On another occasion Coles, Harry and Miss Gladys Latham, who accompanied Jan on the piano during his songs, stayed overnight at an hotel in Holsworthy, where Coles had given one of his one-night stands. It was a centuries-old hotel, with a narrow entrance into the courtyard which served as its carpark. It was a fairly straightforward affair to drive Ole Biskit in when they arrived, but reversing the car out after breakfast the next morning was another matter entirely. The three of them spent a long time in this fruitless pursuit, A. J. C. steering the car (which had a poor lock by any modern standard, and a very fierce clutch) to the encouragements and warnings of the others. Finally they held a committee in the hotel lounge, over a pot of coffee, until one of them said, 'Why not put the car into neutral and push him out?' 'Now why didn't we think of that before?' said A. J. Coles.

Coles explains, in an 'Author's Apology' to *Ole Biskit*, 'the stories in this book were not written with one eye on the Etymologist . . . It has not been written merely to expound the Devon tongue, and if it possess no other interest than that, the book has no justification left.' The book carries, at the end, a useful glossary 'of words and allusions . . . for the better acquaintance of such as are unfamiliar with the Devon dialect'. It includes the following:

SUANT. Regular; even; agreeable. Once in general use. Corn grows *suant*; gentle rain falls *suant*; soldiers march *suant*; a machine works *suant*; music goes *suant* (or not); a preacher preaches *suant* (or otherwise); he even *looks suant*. An admirable word and a great loss to the common language.

TOAD. Almost everything is a toad at some time or another. The Baby's a *bright li'l toad*; Jimmy's a *trying toad*; Poll's a *careless toad*; father's an *unlucky toad*; grandfather's a *knowing ole toad*; the rooks be *terrifying toads*; the cat's a *thieving toad*; and the toad's a frog.

An aunt of mine, who was for a short time an assistant at a Bideford draper's, was once asked by a customer, speaking very quickly: 'Ave 'ee got some dray that won't bissle fer some li'l bits o' toads I've got at 'ome?' Said as if almost one word, it sounds like a foreign language. The woman meant: 'Have you got some trade (material) that won't get dirty for some little bits of toads (her endearing way of describing her offspring) I've got at home?'

Ole Biskit is primarily huge entertainment, and Coles makes full use of every aspect of the car situation in the twelve episodes. Perhaps most amusing are Jan's attempts to resist the family's persuasions to buy a car in the first place.

'There, now. If vather had only got his motor-car he could flip over there with 'ee like winkey.'
Zeeming to me, that's all their idaya, is to zee me go flipping.
Well, and when I had to go out there to Princestown, a day or two agone, there 'twas all over again. A tayjis ole journey that was too. I had to go all out around I dunnaw where to get to it, and all-so-fur back again. Took two whole days to do thik li'l trip. So they all zinged their ole zong again.
'If you only had yer moter-car, zee what difference 'twould-a-made.'
'Ees, I know,' I says. 'I could 'a-flipped there, couldn' I?'
I'm feared of me life to mention I be gwain anyplace. Somebody sure to say, 'If only you had yer car you could flip there.'
'I dersay he'd be handy,' says mother. 'Zee what us could do if us had one.'
'Ees,' I says. 'Jis zee what you could do. You could drive around the coort to veed the pigs and the poultry, and you could flip up to the pump in 'en, and he'd zave yer

legs in gwain back and vore when you was hanging out the washing. I dersay arter a bit you could ride 'n up to bed, and he'd be abble to turn the mangle, and churn the butter, and broom out the back-'ouse arter you'd larned the way to make 'n flip proper.'

Not only is this expression of his growing impatience and fear extremely funny; but, in passing, it may be noticed how much easier the dialect has become to read, at any rate for the non-Devonian. Coles skilfully achieved this while maintaining the idiom and even, to a degree, the accent. There have been some losses: 'Cude' has been restored to 'could', and 'mai' to 'my'; but—a little inconsistently—we still have 'gude' and not 'good'. These are, perhaps, niggling criticisms. We must be thankful for large mercies, and his great achievement is full of them.

Jan is a man of his time, and Chapter Three finds him saying, 'I've got a moter-car out in trap-ouze' (it is a long time before he can get himself to use the unfamiliar word 'garridge'). The fourth chapter is contributed by Mrs Stewer. Finding her husband about to clean the wheels with her dishcloth and furniture polish, she comes out with: 'Not fer Jo. If you wants furniture crame at tenpence-ap'my a bottle you buy it yerzel'.' ('Not fer Jo', an expression whose origin is not touched on in the glossary, means 'Not likely'.) It is in this chapter that the origin of the car's name is explained. Its colour has to be given on a requisite form, and various suggestions are made: 'yaller', 'a soort of dirty yaller', 'stone colour', and 'buff'. Defeated, they call in Sophy Grinnaway, 'her being a dressmaker, and expert as to colours'.

'Why, 'tis biskit colour,' says Sophy, drec'ly.
'Of cou'se 'tis biskit,' says Jane. 'Vancy us not thinking o' that.'
'Well, he takes the biskit anyway,' says the Young Jan, 'so he ought to be that colour.'
So 'Biskit' was wrote down on the paper, and the old toad was called BISKIT from that day forth, and he've gone by that name ever since.

It would be interesting to know how many cars, especially in Devon, have been named after it. When I was a schoolboy, and went for a day's holiday to a friend's father's farm in Somerset, his mother said of their car, 'We always calls it th'Ole Biskit.'

The size of the engine, also needed for the form, is an even greater problem for the Stewer family. They do the all-too-obvious thing and send for the blacksmith, who considers it is 'up two voot, or thereabouts'. But Jan says he reckons 'there mustn' be no "thereabouts" '. The temptation to quote extensively, though great, must be resisted. There is a series of driving lessons, the instructor being the Young Jan, who marries Jan's daughter Jane, and who comes from Kirton (Crediton) Town—surely an echo from Coles's Puddington days. Today Puddington children go to Tiverton or Crediton for their schooling, and the former school is now a village hall. (In March of 1977 I spoke there to the Women's Institute on 'The Art of A. J. Coles: the Immortal Jan Stewer' and attempted a carbon copy of two of the most famous monologues.) The driving lessons are hilarious. Young Jan says, ' 'Twould make a cat laaf to yer you telling to Ole Biskit' for, all unconsciously, Jan has been calling out, 'Com'eer, Biskit, you ole toad, you. Wug back. Biskit, my dear! Stiddy, you ole stoobid. Wug-auf! Woa! Com'eer! Biskit—ah!' But he learns to drive at last, and one day takes his wife, Mrs Snell and Mrs Endycott to Lynton. 'Us be getting up in the mountainous country I should think,' says Jan.

He eventually becomes a competent driver, almost his sole success in the field of the unknown, but throughout he is distrustful of the motives of Ole Biskit, to whom he ascribes an independent and malignant mind: 'Ole Biskit knaw'th. He knaw'th, I tell 'ee, and noting waunt make me believe no other.'

His eventual affection for the car comes almost too late, for this particular 'new-vangled inventation' is all but destroyed by fireworks on the day of Barleycombe Turmut Vair, which is 'orwis the fust Wainsday in November'. After his final journey, Jan writes an affecting poem—the kind of which his creator was just a little too fond—beginning:

You ban't exac'ly hanzum and you ban't exac'ly new; In fact, you'm old and hugly if I mus' say what is true.

It is clear that he thinks of the car in the same terms as he thought of the horses that drew the carrier's van.

Though you'd got old and shaky, yet you always done your best; You zarved me well, Ole Biskit, and you've arned your bit o'rest.

The second half of *Ole Biskit* is devoted to some 'Other Tales', which are among the best of Coles's creations, particularly 'Ned Hannaford Keeps House'. Left to keep house during his wife's absence, Ned finds that it is not as easy as it looks. This emerges as much more than the usual knockabout treatment of a familiar comedy theme, and justifies Betjeman's assessment of Coles as one of the great understanding humorists. One of Ned's workmen finally plucks up enough courage to speak his mind about the unappetising meal Ned has prepared for them.

'Let me tell 'ee maister,' he says, 'that you'm wrong. I *be* hungered. I ab'm had no brekfus, cus what you putt to the taable 's'morning the cat wude'n eat; and I've bin working hard all the voorenoon, as you can zee fer yerzel' if you mind to come out and look. And now I be properly leery; but I cude'n stommick thik ole trade. I wouldn' give it belly-rume, and that's telling of 'ee straight. And I'll tell 'ee zummat else, Mr Annaferd, while us be about it. You'm a very gude weel-wright and you'm a very gude boss. Nobody cude'n wish fer better. But you'm a darn poor cook; and if you daun' know it you ought to be told, and now yu've *been* told. And if I've got to have the sack fer telling of 'ee, well, so 'tis.'

Ned, telling the tale, admits to the moral of so many of these stories—every man to his trade. 'Right?' says Ned. 'Of course 'twas right. And arter I'd lookid the feller straight in the faace fer a minute or two I ketched up the dish o' rabbut stew and emp' the whole lot out o'winder.' It is left to 'li'l Bessie' to take matters in hand, which she does with exemplary competence. Clearly, A. J. Coles was no male chauvinistic pig. The story ends:

And when her'd putt everything to rights her took the other chillern and kiss me gude night and away-do-go-up-over stairs to bed.
 Me and the two chaps sot on a bit, and smocked a pipe o' baccy. And arter a while, I said:
 'Men is men, and women is women.'
 'Did zomebody tell 'ee that, maister?' says George, 'or did you rade it in a book?'
 'Wait a bit,' I says. 'There's a differnce. A man id'n a man till he's full growed, but a wumman's a wumman as soon as her's abble to walk.'

This is pure gold. So is 'The Party', with its observations on people and manners and some remarks on dress. In between the startling appearance upon the rustic scene of the hobble skirt and the coronation of King George VI comes the invention of the wireless, upon which Jan passes his own scathing judgment: 'They ole wireless contraptions which so many volks has got now-a-days, is only what you might call "half-an'-half." They only does their work one way. Like ole Bill Maggs with his missis, you can yer what's being said but you can't putt in a word yerzel.' And he explains that

they there li'l ossylations, arter they've bin all they hunderds o' miles, jugging up and down on they waves, sliding along inzide they wires, pushing and shoving their way in droo your machine, they gets all out o' chune. So bevore they'm any gude to 'ee you've got to chune 'em up agean, like ole Bob Maddick with his viddle up to the dance.
 To do that, you turns around a couple li'l hannles, till you've got'n proper in chune.
 An then you gets the reward fer all yer work and all yer patience. And you can yer the lovely zinging and the muzicking, and 'tis all zo butiful, till the t'other chap

comes along with his ole 'da-da-did-diddy-diddy-da-diddy-da-da,' and then you wants to go and make a vew transgressions of yer awn.

Jan was, in fact, to have some of his tales broadcast on this contraption, and to appear (slightly disguised as someone else, but instantly recognisable) on the later modern miracle of television. But Jan himself never changes or ages. Strangely enough, 'How the Wireless Works' dated very quickly—for it is not only a period piece, it is an anachronism—while the earlier tale of 'Our Electric Light Scheme' does not fade.

In 'History in Ruins', Lias Buzzacott acts as self-appointed guide to parties of visitors to the ruins of Muddlecombe Castle. The garbled history is ingenious, but the humour is contrived; for once A. J. Coles obtrudes and Jan takes a back seat. It is immediately followed by 'Jim Davey and the Rabbit'—as if in atonement, for this is the genuine article.

Ole Biskit contains one prime example of Coles's ability to set a scene. A meeting had been called to discuss the formation of a debating society:

Doctor Jinkins he was the cheerman, up higher end o' the rume, and squire and passen and the rest o' the committee lot, they was sot both sides aw'n, to paust'n up in the matter o' this-yer mind-improving. They was facing towards we, like they would if they was gwain to give intertainment.

Wull then, in the front rove o' cheers there was a vew o' the women-volk what regards theirsel's a bit above the average, like; the wives of the big varmers, and the skulemissis, and Tilda Grinnaway the dressmaker, and Miss Peters what lived up to Lunnon fer upperds o' ten years and made nothing o' seeing the King and Quane driving about in the park.

And then come two roves with nobody, only cheers. And arter that the varmers what belonged to the wives in the front sates. And then there was two more roves empty. Then come the maidens what did'n want to get too fur away from the chaps, and behind they was the chaps what did'n want to be too fur away from the maidens but had'n got the face to zit bezide 'em.

In the back sates of all was the rest o'the women from the village with their baabies. And they told each other they was thankful *their* minds did'n want improving like they what had the chick to poke theirsel's right up in the front.

Stood up at the back was the men what wanted to be near the door in case the meetin' shude last on till closing-time. And out in the lobby was the policeman where he could be handy to both plaaces.

Lias and Betty, the first of his books that can properly be called a novel, was published in 1938, having first appeared in serial form in the *Western Weekly News*. It is a romance pure and simple—the familiar phrase is deliberately chosen—with Muddlecombe as its setting and one of its best-loved characters, Lias Buzzacott (a sort of Devonshire Sam Weller), its hero. It also contains most of the other familiar villagers: Tom Zalter and the bus that succeeded the carrier's van; 'Mrs Snell, round and cheerful;

Mrs Endycott, thin an' crabbid; Ned Annaferd, the wheelwright'; and, of course, Sophy Grinnaway, known as the "Muddlecombe Daily News". Farmer Urferd, mean and grasping, Jan Stewer devotees have met before, but not, I think his daughter Betty. She alone of all the characters fails to come over as a distinct personality; she is a doll, merely a foil for Lias's love affair. A. J. Coles could describe middle-aged and older women but his young girls never come to life. The book is eminently readable, as is anything he wrote, with that acute psychological insight into the motives and reactions of these people to a given situation which by this time was second nature to him. Jan tells the story, but plays no more significant part than that of a sympathetic observer. A. J. Coles, with the non-west-country reader in mind, plays down the dialect, and perhaps falls between two stools in this folksy tale.

The best sections of *Lias and Betty* are the two introductions, which deserve full quotation.

> The story of Lias Buzzacott and Betty Urferd was first told in odd bits and pieces over a period of several years, by my other half, Jan Stewer, in the *Western Weekly News*. In compliance with many appeals he has now written this romance in a single volume. Out of consideration for those unfamiliar with the native tongue, I have taken the liberty of modifying the dialect in some instances for greater ease of the narrative than as a representation of the dialect. For any defection of the vernacular, therefore, or for apparent inconsistencies in spelling, the blame is mine. A. J. COLES.

> A lot o' volks has axed me to putt down what I knaws about Lias Buzzacott and Betty Urferd into a buke. I ban't much of a feller to write a buke. I reckon it takes somebody a bit more eddicative than what I be to do that. However, I've wraut it down so-well as I can in me awn lingo. Whatever tettyvatin' tother feller have done to it is he's look-out. JAN STEWER.

Coles has said, which I often suspected, that there came a time when it was difficult for him to write other than in dialect form, so ingrained had the habit become. Meaning to write 'I saw you last week', he would find himself writing 'I zee'd 'ee las' wik'.

The second novel, *The Shop With Two Windows*, came out in 1952. Here the dialect, except in conversations, is reduced even further, so much so that it might as well have been abandoned altogether. It is in the same genre as its predecessor, but has less incident and could easily have been compressed into a short story. However its three main characters, Andy Clampitt, Bessie Kelland and Aunt Clara, come to life; and the heroine (Bessie) is convincing as a young woman of strong willpower and determination.

The two novels are collectors' pieces for Jan Stewer's many devotees, but are not vintage material. The invention is beginning to flag; the zenith has been passed. *The Shop With Two Windows* has a certain rustic charm but sails dangerously close to the Mummerzet whimsy Coles had hitherto successfully avoided. But in his penultimate volume, *On the Moor of a Night*, Coles wisely returned to his natural milieu. Here we step back with relief to hear again—because this is a collection which includes much old material—the authentic dialect tone. It is an uneven, mixed book, with some informed and intriguing 'Charitable Notes' at the end: 'A few Observations by the Author on some of the less obvious words occurring in this Book; for the Greater Comfort of such Readers as may not have had the Privilege of a Devon rustic Background or Upbringing.' The following is an example:

abroad—Used in a much narrower sense than 'oversea' (which would be 'furrin parts'). For instance, to repair a clock or machine, one would need to 'take 'n abroad'—ie to pieces. We break a plate or a dish *abroad* ('He was broke all abroad to shords'). Incidentally, we also *break* a newspaper or a book *abroad*. A person who has grown stout had 'vailed (fallen) *abroad*'. To reduce a log to firewood we would 'kanck 'en (knock it) *abroad*'. *en*—Adjectival ending; almost rare in 'bettermost' circles with a few exceptions, such as golden hair, wooden spoon, leaden sky, woollen socks, and so on; but very well preserved in our parish. We have a crippled man with a *timbern* leg who wears a *clothen* coat with *bonen* buttons and a *leathern* belt. His garden has an *oaken* gate with *stonen* gate-posts. His wife uses a *tinnen* kettle, a *cloamen* jug, a *timbern* spoon, and has a *silvern* thimble in a *brassen* box. Sometimes she brings home from the shop a *boughten* cake in a *papern* bag.

'A Queen's Garments' is characteristic—all about 'the shindy that was kicked up to Raxun Village, over choosin' the Carnival Quane'. 'Robbery in the Parish' is a cleverly told detective story. It is in dialect, of course, and the setting is the usual rustic one, but there is something almost cheeky about the way he throws this one in to demonstrate his versatility. 'See? I can write a good detective yarn if I want to.' And so he can. The book also contains some short dramatic sketches, but none of any great merit. There is (probably by request) a reprint of a very old poem, 'Out of the Darkness', which has a decided 'Christmas Day at the Workhouse' ring about it. It is, however, in the familiar delivery that the book's strength lies. The last tale, 'Jan's Wedding Present', ends thus:

And bim-bye I said to mother, 'Do 'ee think 'twill fit 'ee all right? Did'n you ought to try 'en on in case he won't do?'
  That was all her wanted. Her got up from the zupper table an' went out of the rume like a long-dog. When her come back her had on her woolly cardigan.
  'How do 'ee like it, mother?' I says.
  ' 'Tis bevore Mrs Row's, I reckon,' her says. And what could any wumman wish for better'n that?

EIGHT

The Immortal Jan Stewer

A. J. Coles had a number of homes. Jan Stewer's homes cannot be counted. It is probable that clergymen with a west-country background do not, as traditionally do their colleagues, turn to Agatha Christie or some other writer of detective fiction as a refreshing change from theological studies or sermon preparation. They are as likely to pull out of their shelves one or other of the several volumes in which (in large part) the reincarnation of Ned Knowles is imperishably enshrined. Particularly in Devon, Somerset and Cornwall will his philosophical observations and misadventures continue to be read. But exiles all over the world, not only in midland and northern parts of the British Isles, still open the pages of *In Chimley Corner* and have a quiet chuckle before retiring to bed. Styles of humour are ever-changing; last year's television comedies are already beginning to date. Jan's tales are imperishable.

A. J. Coles's last home was appropriately enough a caravan hidden by Devon trees in Pathfinder Village, Tedburn St Mary, on the Exeter-Okehampton road. In 1951, when he went there, he was one of the first inhabitants of this growing 'village' of luxury caravans. It was close to Five Mile Farm where he and the family opened the 'Jan Stewer Tay Gardens'—a touch of *Agatha's Heaven* here—and of which there still exists a photograph, taken with members of the family and others in full make-up as Muddlecombians (Jan dominates the scene).

While at Pathfinder, where Coles lived with his wife, his dialect writings continued for some time and then gradually slowed to a stop. He continued to make intermittent stage appearances, but no longer with full Jan Stewer make-up. Sometimes he relied merely on the beard, sometimes he abandoned even that—such a master of mimicry needed no artificial aids to create an illusion. He had, in his time, the aid of grease paint, whiskers and wig, full costume and often the assistance of two sons and two daughters; he was proud of the family being part of the act. But he could do the thing alone, and did so at first (and latterly) in church and village halls, sometimes with Stuart Keen showing the Dartmoor film.

It was at Pathfinder, in 1961, that Mr and Mrs A. J. Coles celebrated their diamond wedding anniversary. This was also the year of her death (she was older than he) at the age of ninety-one. They lived in what was virtually one L-shaped caravan, made out of two, with access from his to her sleeping-quarters. In the morning she would make the tea, using an electric kettle by the side of her bed, and would press a bell which rang in his caravan; they would then have their tea together. One morning the bell did not ring, and he went in to find she had died in the night. In her larder was the Sunday joint she had cooked the day before and the remains of the roast potatoes; she had also made an apple pie and four fruit jellies in case any of her children should visit them, as they often did.

Coles's health remained good, and his only prescribed 'medicine' was three pints of liquid a day. As the doctor had omitted to define what form the liquid should take, he promptly decided upon beer. He stayed on at Pathfinder, but continued to drive a car. On 17 July 1962, he wrote in a letter to me:

I am sorry this reply is so long delayed but I have been away a good deal lately—Blandford, Birmingham (to my daughter's), Malvern; not to mention Torquay . . . The new domestic household duties—cooking, cleaning, scouring saucepans etc. absorb so much of my time that I find myself putting off till tomorrow many of the things I had 'ordained' doing today.

He was then eighty-six.

In the hard winter of 1962-3, he left St Austell, where he had been staying with his daughter Mary and her husband, to motor back to Tedburn St Mary. On the evening of 8 December 1962, he wrote this letter:

It is 7.45 and I have just sat down. My only previous recline into a sitting position since I got up, was, as well as I can remember, about half way down the road from the village shop; said road being one long stretch of glassy snow. The rest of the day I have spent in endeavouring to persuade the various waste pipes to waste. Up to the present I still have the same water in the sink, wash basin and bath etc. as this time yesterday.

As practically everything out of doors is hidden under two feet of snow, thawing pipes which are solid throughout their length is . . . unrewarding. (I thought of 'unrewarding' just in time!) Most people here have had their pipes frozen but I am in a class by myself in that I have a cracked lavatory pan. A new one I understand is coming tomorrow.

The journey up was an experience I'd hate to have again, but having safely accomplished it, I'm not sorry to have seen for myself the weather forecast in actual practice.

The roads through Cornwall were quite reasonably good. At Liskeard I took bad advice. The Policeman on point duty said the going was all right via Okehampton. Again, as far as Tavistock the going was quite good. From there on it was unbelievable. I was soon travelling in a one car width lane with a white wall either side the height of the car.

This went on for miles and endless miles—until in fact joining the Launceston road. At a point just after Mary Tavy, I met a convoy of two cars and a great lorry. With the assistance of two pushing and two more giving me contrary instructions I slithered back a long distance to find room to pass. Altogether I was just on forty minutes at this stop.

I was looking forward all the way in hopes I would make the main road at the Launceston junction anticipating that it would be clear like those as far as Tavistock. As a matter of fact the whole length of road from there to Tedburn was incredible. There is no resemblance to a road. The snow is frozen in lumps, humps, mounds and ridges; nowhere was it safe to get above second gear and 10 m.p.h. was the top limit. At the top of the hill before Okehampton, I joined the queue, switched off and read for another forty minutes. There were two more long stops before reaching the town where divers lorries were disentangled.

On the rise out of Sticklepath there were two stops of 11 and 14 minutes. At Crockernwell the block lasted half an hour. While travelling, the hills and valleys in the road surface meant that one did almost as much sideways as forwards, and it wasn't only the old—let's see, old what was it? I forget. Anyway, nobody was daring to move above the 10 m.p.h.

I will admit that had I known what it was going to be like, I wouldn't have taken it on and you would have been stuck with me.

His death was as sudden and dramatic as his birth. He was a keen bowler; and through this interest had formed a firm friendship with a Mr and Mrs Les Dear of Cricketts Cross, Ferndown, Dorset. Not unnaturally, they found his company congenial. The Dears always insisted on coming to Tedburn for him and driving him to their home. On the evening of 18 August 1965, when they had done this, he told them that he was going for a walk—and he died as a result of being in collision with a van on the Bournemouth-Ringwood road.

The evening paper carried the inevitable heading, 'Tragic Death of "Jan Stewer" '. Yet it was wrong on two counts. A. J. Coles always had that fear which haunts so many old people, that he might become senile or in some way a burden to others. This did not happen, and can the sudden death of a man in his ninetieth year and in full possession of all his faculties be described accurately as 'tragic'?

Nor was it the death of Jan Stewer. He goes on playing that immortal cricket match, he still has trouble filling in the census paper, and whatever forms of heating and lighting nuclear energy may provide for homes of the future, Jan will regale generations to come with the story of 'this-yer 'lectristical light'. Jan lives still, contentedly, in a period of our history when social distinctions are accepted without rancour or sense of inferiority—and can refer, with a glorious and complete unawareness of the implications of his words, to 'squire and his laady, and passen and his wive, and Doctor Jinkins and his missis'.

It is a truism that we live in a period of transition; it is said that Adam made the same observation to Eve. But Jan does not change. He still has the true countryman's slowness of speech and fondness for detail; the modern journalistic technique of telegrammatic speech holds no attraction for him. He takes his time reaching the main point, as well he may in the timeless world in which he lives. Good listeners will find their patience richly rewarded as he launches out on one of the narratives from his ample repertoire:

Only one day las' wik, my missis had to go to Kirton Town on a matter o' business. Well, down there where the Young Jan comes from, that's where 'twas. Las' Vridy I think 'twas. Or Zaturday, I dunnaw which. Must a-bin Vridy. No, 'twad'n. 'Twas Zaturday, I know 'twas, cus the nex' day was Zindy, and there wad'n no trains to come back by . . .

Chronology of Works

9 March 1900. The first article signed by 'Jan Stewer' appears in the *Devon and Exeter Gazette*.

Between 1900 and 1910. *In A Devonshire Carrier's Van*: Tales told in the Devon Dialect (three series) published by Western Morning News Co. Ltd.

c. 1902. Publication of *Jan Stewer's Demshur Buke*.

c. 1922. Publication of *Jan Stewer at Home and Abroad*, written during the First World War.

1925. *Ole Biskit* published by Besley & Copp, Exeter; later republished by Herbert Jenkins and Westaway Books.

Between 1927 and 1935. *The Cat and the Pigeons, Mr Furlinger* and *Agatha's Heaven* (plays) written and produced.

c. 1928. *In Chimley Corner* published by Herbert Jenkins; later republished by Westaway Books.

1930. *A Parcel of Ol' Crams* published by Herbert Jenkins; later republished by Westaway Books.

1931. *Yap* published by Herbert Jenkins, later republished by Westaway Books.

10 August 1931. First night of *Barnet's Folly* at the Plymouth Repertory Theatre.

1932. A. J. Coles first plays the part of George Growsell in *Barnet's Folly* at Torquay Pavilion.

14 February 1935. First night of *Barnet's Folly* at the Haymarket Theatre, London.

1938. *Lias and Betty* published by Herbert Jenkins, later republished by Westaway Books.

1949. *On the Moor of a Night* published by Westaway Books.

1952. *The Shop with Two Windows* published by Westaway Books.

Index

The names of books, plays, etc, are in italics; monologues and short stories are given in single quotes, and the names of fictional places in double quotes.

Agatha's Heaven (play), 68
Alford, Winifred, 50-1
All Along, Down Along (film), 74
Ayliff, H. K., 70

Balchin, Charles, 29
"Barleycombe", 26
Barnet's Folly (play), 67, 68-73
Bath and West Show film, 75
'The Best Lies Deepest', 35
Boer War, 20-1
Bovey Tracey, 57, 65
Bowey, J. S., 68
Boxer Rising, 24
'Boxing Day at Muddlecombe', 37
'Breathing Room Only', 85
Bristol, 16

Calvert, Phyllis, 70
The Cat and Pigeons (play), 67
Chaplin, Charles, 13
Charity appearances, 46-7
Chaucer, Geoffrey, 58-9, 60, 63-4
Coles family, 14
Coles, Albert John ("Jan Stewer")
  acting ability, 73
  army service, 15, 26-9
  birth and upbringing, 12
  changeable temperament, 42
  choice of pseudonym, 17
  comparison between creator and creation, 39-40
  death, 98
  Devon family background, 14
  first published story, 17
  first stage appearance, 46
  inspiration for stage make-up, 45
  marriage, 14
  moves to Torquay, 26
  political affiliations, 41, 65
  prodigious output, 30
  schoolmaster, 16
  at night school, 65
  at Poltimore and Bovey Tracey, 56-7, 60
  at Teignmouth, 54-6
Coles, Colin, 14-15, 68, 88
Coles, Florence
  death, 97
  marriage, 14
  role in family, 42, 43
  similarity to fictional wife, 40
Coles, Harry, 30, 88
  as accompanying pianist, 48
  birth, 14
Coles, Joan, 15, 51
Coles, Mary, 15, 68
Collected stories, 32
Crompton, Richmal, 31

Devon and Exeter Gazette
  invites contributions from "Jan Stewer", 17, 19-20
  monologues reprinted, 32
Dialect
  derivations of words, 60-4
  teaching in schools, 57-9
Dickens, Charles, 86
Donat, Robert, 74
Dunsford, Percy, 69

Edward VIII, King (later Duke of Windsor), 51
'Every Man to His Trade', 82

Film commentaries, 74-5
'For the Good of the Cause', 85
Furler, Jack, 66, 67

Gateway to Heaven (film), 75
Gibb, Keith, 74
Gibson, Chloe, 69, 70
Gratwicke, G. F., 17, 19, 46
  gives contract for weekly feature, 19-20
Grendon Players, 67-8
Grimsdick, John, 78-9
Guest, Alik, 52
'The Gurt Romance', 87

'The Haughty Maid', 79
'Have We Lived Before?, 85
Haymarket Theatre, 68, 69-70
'History in Ruins', 93
'How the Wireless Works', 93
'The Hunt Dinner', *see* 'The Swell Dinner'

Illustrated Sporting and Dramatic News, 73
In a Devonshire Carrier's Van (book), 25, 32-8
In Chimley Corner (book), 78

Jackson, Sir Harry, 69
'Jan and the Census Paper', 15, 18, 52, 79
Jan Stewer at Home and Abroad (book), 32
Jan Stewer's Demshur Buke, 32
'Jan's Adventures in London', 83
'Jan's Fiddle', 79
'Jan's First and Last Cricket Match', 41, 52, 80
'Jan's Paper-hanging', 40-1
'Jan's Wedding Present', 95
Jenkins, Herbert, publisher, 78
'The Jibbing Moter', 36
'Jim Davey and the Rabbit', 93
'Judgment', 86

Keen, Stuart, 73, 74, 96
Knowles, Ned, 24, 25, 45

Latham, Gladys, 88
Lias and Betty (book), 93-4
'Lias in Town', 86
'The Likeness Taker', 86
Limbert, Roy, 69, 70

Malvern Festival, 74
'The Man Who Never Told a Lie', 34
Mary, Queen, 51-2
Michael, Ralph, 70
Mid Devon Advertiser, 76
Mr Furlinger (play), 68
"Muddlecombe", 19

'Ned Hannaford Keeps House', 91-2

Old Peter (ventriloquist's dummy), 46
Ole Biskit (book), 85, 87-91, 93
On the Moor of A Night (book), 14, 95
'On the Underground', 83
'The 'Orrible Skirt', 31
'Our Electric Light Scheme', 80, 93
'Out Come Mother and Me', 44
'Out of the Darkness', 95

A Parcel of Ol' Crams (book), 83
'A Parcel of Trumpery', 85
'The Party', 92
Pathfinder Village, 96
Phillpotts, Eden, 37
Pianists, 48-51
'Pity the Poor Foreigner', 33
Play Pictorial (magazine), 73
Plymouth Repertory Theatre, 69
Poltimore, 56
Puddington, 15, 16

'A Queen's Garments', 95

Radio broadcasts, 93
"Raxun", 26
'The Resolving Staircase', 83
'Reuben Ley in the Higher Circle', 32
Revel Day (play), 65-7
Richards, Frank, 31
'Robbery in the Parish', 95

Sanders, Leslie, 69
The School Bell (magazine), 16-17
The Shop with Two Windows (book), 94
'The Singing Match', 85
'The Song of the Settle', 79
'Speech on a Church Clock', 83
Sprague, William, 45
Stage appearances, 43-53
Stephens family, 14
"Stewer, Jan", *see* Coles, Albert John
'The Swell Dinner', 23, 29, 32, 79, 84

'Tales from the Carrier's Cart', 84-5
Teignmouth, 54-5
Television broadcasts, 93
36 Club, 73

'Tom Zalter's Day's Pleasure', 85
Torbay News, 76

Watson, Horace, 69-70
'The Wedding', 86
"Week St Agnes", 26
Western Weekly News, 20, 31
   serialisation of *Lias and Betty*, 93, 94
'What About a Little Drop o' Cider?', 45
'When Jan Played Football', 83
'When Mother and Me Joined In', 44-5
'Will Brewer and the Boots', 80
'The Working Model', 85
World War I, 26
   stage performances during, 51
Wreford, Charles, 57

Yap, 43, 85